The Complete Book of

# Les Misérables

The Complete Book of

# Les Misérables

EDWARD BEHR

Arcade Publishing · New York

*By the same author*

THE ALGERIAN PROBLEM
"ANYONE HERE BEEN RAPED AND SPEAKS ENGLISH?"
GETTING EVEN
THE LAST EMPEROR
HIROHITO: BEHIND THE MYTH

FIRST U.S. EDITION

The following previously copyrighted material is used
by permission:

English lyrics © 1985 Alain Boublil Music Ltd.
All dramatic performance rights worldwide in the musical
"Les Misérables" reserved to Cameron Mackintosh (Overseas)
Ltd, of 1 Bedford Square, London WC1B 3RA.
"Les Misérables" logo © 1986 Cameron Mackintosh
(Overseas) Ltd.
"Les Misérables" graphics designed by Dewynters PLC,
London.
"You" and "Ten Little Bullets" © 1984 James Fenton.

*Library of Congress Cataloging-in-Publication Data*
Behr, Edward, 1926–
    The complete book of Les misérables / Edward Behr.
        p.        cm.
    ISBN 1-55970-033-5 (hc)
    ISBN 1-55970-156-0 (pb)
    1. Hugo, Victor, 1802–1885 — Adaptations.  2. Hugo, Victor,
1802–1885 — Film and video adaptations.  3. Hugo, Victor, 1802–1885 —
Musical settings.  4. Boublil, Alain.  [1. Hugo, Victor,
1802–1885.  Misérables.  2. Schönberg, Claude-Michel.  Misérables.]
I. Title
PQ2286.B4      1989
843'.7 — dc20                                                    89-15093

Published in the United States by Arcade Publishing,
Inc., New York, by arrangement with Little, Brown and Company

Distributed by Little, Brown and Company

10 9 8 7 6 5 4 3 2 1

Designed by Peter Guy

PRINTED IN THE UNITED STATES OF AMERICA

# Contents

# Acknowledgments

I would like to thank all those who talked to me at great (and sometimes repeated) length, answered all questions patiently and frankly and without whom this book would not have been possible: Alain Boublil, John Caird, James Fenton, Dudu Fisher, David Hersey, Herbert Kretzmer, Patti LuPone, Gillian Lynne, Cameron Mackintosh, Patricia Macnaughton, John Napier, Andreane Neofitou, Trevor Nunn, Claude-Michel Schönberg, Julian Slade, Colm Wilkinson and many, many others.

Thanks also to James Fenton for allowing me to reproduce the lyrics of 'You' and 'Ten Little Bullets' and – last but not least – to Victor Hugo himself, to whom all those involved in the *Les Misérables* musical-theatre undertaking owe a huge, unrepayable debt.

Photographs unless otherwise stated by Michael Le Poer Trench.

1772 Birth of Sophie-Françoise Trébuchet, Victor Hugo's mother.

1773 Birth of Léopold-Sigisbert Hugo, Victor Hugo's father.

1789 French Revolution begins.

1792 First French Republic proclaimed.

1792–95 The republican 'Convention', ending in Robespierre's 'terror'.

1793 Louis XVI executed. The 'Chouans' (royalist Breton insurgents) begin their full-scale civil war against the republican French Government. Léopold-Sigisbert Hugo, an officer in the republican army, is posted to Brittany as part of the repressive peace-keeping force.

1795–99 'Le Directoire', the first post-revolution Government.

1796 Léopold-Sigisbert Hugo, on patrol, meets Sophie-Françoise Trébuchet, a Royalist, verifies her identity papers, searches her parents' farm – and falls in love with her.

1797 Marriage, in Paris, of Sophie Trébuchet and Léopold-Sigisbert Hugo.

1798 Birth of Abel Hugo, Victor Hugo's elder brother (who dies, insane, 1855).

1799–1804 The 'Consulat'. Bonaparte takes command.

1802 Birth of Victor-Marie Hugo.

1803 Léopold-Sigisbert Hugo posted to Elba, in disgrace, remains there with his three small sons (Eugène, the youngest, is born in 1803) while Sophie Hugo remains in Paris, and is befriended by General Victor Lahorie, her husband's former Commanding Officer. Léopold and Sophie drift apart; he takes up with Catherine Thomas (a nurse), and begins living with her. Sophie Hugo finally joins her husband in Elba briefly, but they quarrel constantly.

1804–15 French Empire; rise and fall of the Napoleonic Empire, ending with the battle of Waterloo.

1804 Napoleon crowns himself at Notre Dame; French Empire proclaimed.

Sophie Hugo and her three children return to Paris, settling at 24 rue de Clichy. General Lahorie, now retired and wanted by the police for plotting against Napoleon, lives at no. 19.

1807 Léopold Hugo promoted colonel and posted to Naples, where he makes a favourable impression on Napoleon's younger brother, Joseph.

1808 Joseph Bonaparte is made King of Spain by Napoleon. Léopold Hugo follows the French King to Spain at the latter's request, and gets a lucrative staff appointment.

1811 Sophie Hugo makes one last attempt to resume marital relations with Léopold, and joins him, with her family, in Spain. Léopold hears of his wife's affair with Lahorie and sues for divorce. Sophie and her children return to Paris a few months later.

1812 Lahorie is executed for plotting Napoleon's downfall.

1814 Back in France, General Léopold Hugo distinguishes himself at the siege of Thionville. Sophie Hugo sues him for maintenance.

1815 France becomes a monarchy once more under Louis XVIII. General Léopold Hugo mistakenly hopes that by rallying to Louis XVIII *in extremis* he will be able to stay in the army. He is retired on half-pay.

1815–24 Reign of Louis XVIII.

1820 Victor Hugo's *Ode on the Death of the Duc de Berri* attracts the attention of the Court. Louis XVIII sends him 500 francs.

1821 Death of Sophie Hugo. Léopold Hugo marries his mistress, Catherine Thomas.

# and Times of Victor Hugo

1822  Victor Hugo marries childhood sweetheart Adèle Foucher.

1823  Birth of Victor Hugo's first son, Léopold-Victor.

1824–30  Reign of Charles X.

1825  Victor Hugo awarded the Légion d'honneur for services to literature.

1826  Birth of Victor Hugo's second son, Charles-Victor.

1827  Birth of Victor Hugo's third son, François-Victor.

1828  Death of General Léopold-Sigisbert Hugo.

1829  Birth of Victor Hugo's first daughter, Adèle.

1830  Première of Victor Hugo's play, *Hernani*, interrupted by fist-fights between admirers and detractors. Birth of second daughter, Léopoldine.

1830–48  Reign of King Louis Philippe.

1831  Victor Hugo publishes *Notre-Dame de Paris*.

1832  Hugo meets Juliette Drouet. Funeral of General Lamarque – hero to workers and students – degenerates into riots, and the barricades later described in the third volume of *Les Misérables*.

1836  Applies for membership of Académie Française; fails.

1839  Second Académie Française election attempt again ends in failure.

1841  Victor Hugo finally elected to the Académie Française.

1843  Death of Léopoldine Hugo.

1845  Victor Hugo starts writing *Les Misérables*.

1848–51  Reign of King Louis Philippe ends with uprising and Louis Napoleon becomes President of the Second French Republic.

2 December 1851  Louis Napoleon dissolves Parliament, is proclaimed President with full powers for ten years, ratified by a plebiscite. Victor Hugo leaves hastily for Brussels.

1852  Louis Napoleon proclaims himself Emperor as Napoleon III. Victor Hugo settles first in Jersey then in Guernsey.

1852–70  Emperor Napoleon III establishes cordial relations with Britain. Hugo vows not to set foot on French soil till his removal.

1853  Victor Hugo publishes poetry, *Les Châtiments*, to great acclaim.

1856  Publication of more poetry, *Les Contemplations*.

1861  Victor Hugo completes *Les Misérables*.

1862  *Les Misérables* published in Paris and Brussels.

1868  Adèle Hugo dies.

1870  Franco-Prussian war ends with disastrous battle of Sedan. Napoleon III flees France and settles in England.

October  Victor Hugo returns to Paris, is elected a Member of Parliament by the Parisians.

1871  Victor Hugo resigns from Parliament; following the death of his son, Charles, he goes to Brussels to settle the family inheritance.

April–May  Paris 'Commune' uprising, soon crushed, leads to appalling carnage and repression.

August  From Brussels, Hugo protests against the Belgian Government's refusal to give fleeing 'Communards' status of political exiles. His Brussels house is stoned and he is declared *persona non grata* in Belgium, moving to Luxembourg, returning briefly to Paris, then to Guernsey to write *Quatre-Vingt-Treize*.

1875  Victor Hugo settles permanently in Paris, and is appointed Senator.

1882  Death of Juliette Drouet.

23 May 1885  Victor Hugo dies.

1 June  State funeral attended by over three million people.

# The Father of
# Les Misérables

Victor Hugo defies classification. Few authors have achieved his kind of fame or put such a personal imprint on the century in which they lived.

Hugo was France's most famous poet, playwright and essayist and also a prolific novelist – *Les Misérables* being only one of a dozen major works of fiction. He was also a pamphleteer, a compulsive letter-writer and diary-keeper, a politician, a prophet and above all, perhaps, a Christian moralist, reviled by the Vatican in his lifetime but a source of inspiration for generations of future reformers and social activists.

He became a celebrity when he was still a teenager – a hero to the workers while at the same time mingling with kings and chiefs of state on equal terms – probably the first example of the modern media megastar. His vision of the future was surprisingly accurate: he was, arguably, the first male feminist writer as well as the first advocate of a democratic United States of Europe, also playing a leading role in shaping the chequered course of his beloved France from dictatorship to democracy.

For all his cosmopolitanism, and influence on literary and political movements throughout the world (Marxism would not have been the same without him) he was quintessentially French, in his outlook, his whimsy, his prickly individualism – and his sexuality. In every way he was larger than life, and in many ways he was outrageous, a mass of contradictions. The feminist writer was also a rake, the passionate humanist, in his youth and early middle age at least, a snob and arrant conservative, the lyrical, romantic exponent of idealised love capable of crude, scatological outbursts and confessions. He was, as his assiduous biographer, Hubert Juin, noted, 'a kind of miracle, multiple, unique . . . a monster.'

His self-promotion, in the pre-mass-media, pre-television age, was masterly, his appetite, both for fame and food, voracious. Detractors claimed that he was nothing more than an astute political opportunist and literary careerist, tailoring his views to the changing circumstances of nineteenth-century France, and it's certainly true that he began his writing career with fawning odes to the French Royal Family, in later life tried to suppress some of his more reactionary parliamentary speeches, and that his concern for humanity, though real and all-consuming, was emotional rather than political. It stemmed from a profoundly romantic belief in the existence of an all-high

Divine Providence rewarding the good and punishing the evil. 'The priests hate me', he wrote, 'because I poach on their preserves.'

The whole of Victor Hugo's life was as improbably romantic as the subplots in *Les Misérables*, and if it's true that childhood is the crucible that determines our later development, his was to be richly inspirational: in an age when travel was difficult, and restricted to horse-drawn carts and carriages, he crossed and recrossed Europe as an 'army brat' with his mother, first to Elba and back, then to Naples and back, and finally to Madrid.

Spain, at the time, was up in arms against Napoleon's brutal French military occupation, and Hugo's father, an officer in Napoleon's army, was part of the occupation force that tried to keep the patriotic nationalists at bay. Like other, later, 'gauleiters', General Léopold-Sigisbert Hugo indulged in wholesale plunder, and felt no guilt for the war crimes he committed in the name of order. One of young Victor Hugo's earliest memories was that of Spanish 'partisans', conveniently branded as 'brigands', strung up on either side of country roads – a Goyaesque horror vision, seen through the eyes of a child. All of Victor Hugo's early travels took place against this cruel backdrop.

Hugo witnessed another war at close quarters: the domestic feud between his mother, Sophie, the Breton Royalist, and her estranged husband, Léopold-Sigisbert, the increasingly unstable revolutionary soldier turned mediocre general. It began practically from the time of Victor's birth. He had, in fact, been conceived during one of his parents' many attempts at reconciliation; they never lasted long.

The upright, Catholic, Madame Hugo soon became the devoted mistress of her husband's former commanding officer, General Victor Fanneau Lahorie, carrying on an affair, from 1803, behind the unsuspecting Léopold's back for years. Lahorie was also a Breton, and, despite his distinguished service in the early Napoleonic wars, was bitterly opposed to Napoleon's later excesses and increasingly costly, totalitarian imperial megalomania; Lahorie was later involved in plots against Napoleon, and became an outcast, forced to assume aliases and disguises – on the run from stern political police as relentless as any Javert. Léopold Hugo had taken a mistress soon after Victor Hugo's birth, and sued for divorce. The bickering over his family's support costs lasted for years.

In his childhood and early adolescence, Victor Hugo sided wholeheartedly with his mother, and the kindly, generous Lahorie (sentenced to death and executed in 1812 after taking part in a particularly inept plot to overthrow Napoleon) became a father-figure, whose loss Hugo would mourn almost as intensely as his mother did.

From the moment he started school, it was clear that young

Victor Hugo was something of a prodigy, excelling in physics, mathematics and philosophy as well as French literature, mastering Latin and Greek with ease, translating Virgil, Horace and Lucan into elegant French hexameters that far surpassed his teachers' clumsy models. Writing poetry was as natural to him as breathing, his inventiveness and mastery of language effortless. France's most famous living poet at that time was Chateaubriand, and at the age of fifteen, it became Victor Hugo's goal to be 'Chateaubriand or nothing'.

In the conventional, stylistically strait-jacketed academic tradition of the period, Hugo submitted odes, wrote to order on themes such as 'the happiness procured by study', and was rewarded, as was the custom, by royal patronage. Louis XVIII, good-natured, enormously fat, a caricatural monarch with an even more caricatural, sycophantic court, prided himself on his literary taste and support of the arts. Victor Hugo's first writer's earnings, at eighteen, came in the form of a 500-franc purse from the King for his ode on the death of the Duc de Berri, murdered by Louvel, a republican revolutionary.

In 1819 Hugo began contributing poems to the *Conservateur littéraire* and *Drapeau blanc*, both royalist papers, and received the ultimate poet's accolade: an invitation from Chateaubriand himself. He found France's greatest living poet to be an unbearably pompous bore, whose praise of young Hugo's poetry was double-edged: 'There are things no other poet of his time could have written,' he told Hugo. 'Unfortunately, my age and experience give me the right to be frank, and I tell you candidly there are parts that I like less; but that which is fine is fine.'

Victor Hugo was asked if he had been pleased to meet the master. 'Yes,' said Hugo, 'especially to leave.' But to be a member of Chateaubriand's court was the next best thing to being close to that of Louis XVIII. Hugo duly danced attendance on the great man, listened to Chateaubriand interminably reading his own poetry, even watched him bathe and dress. The charmed Chateaubriand referred to him as 'the sublime child', and the label stuck, but Madame Chateaubriand, who jealously restricted the number of visitors her husband received, treated Hugo as an upstart. Knowing how poor he was, she found great pleasure in extracting money from him for charitable causes. 'It was', Hugo noted, 'the only time I ever saw her smile.' It would all be grist to Hugo the novelist's mill.

As Hugo was later lucidly to admit, 'I was born in a class which made me a Royalist from childhood, before I knew what I was.' His royalist phase, even by French nineteenth-century standards, was excessive: he wrote poems attacking Voltaire, anti-royalist poets, free-thinkers, and was rewarded with a small (1000-franc) annual stipend from the Royal privy purse. Privately, Hugo was dismayed. He had hoped for more.

He also fell head over heels in love. Sixteen-year-old Adèle Foucher was the daughter of a senior civil servant in the French War Ministry, a loyal servant of the Crown. The Fouchers and Sophie Hugo were friends, and the two families spent more and more time together in the grace-and-favour apartment occupied by the Fouchers. There was a wholly practical reason for this: the Foucher quarters were well heated – at government expense – coal was expensive, and Madame Hugo's allowance from her estranged husband wretchedly small.

But Sophie Hugo had high hopes for her son, already a poet with a growing reputation as an adolescent prodigy, and she broke off the love match. Marriage to Adèle, she told Victor, would occur 'only over my dead body'. Rather than break with his mother, the filial Victor Hugo agreed not to see Adèle again, though he dogged her steps, spying on her, in constant torment.

He did, however, continue to write to her, and his lingering, unhappy love affair fuelled his talents as a romantic poet. He was now a regular contributor to the *Conservateur littéraire*, submitting an endless stream of poems, essays, literary criticism and 'mood' pieces. He was beginning to acquire a national reputation, and now, for the first time, embarked on a novel. *Han d'Islande* was a derivative, over-written piece of work, in the style of Walter Scott, whom Hugo had just discovered in translation. The theme, however, was real, and close to his heart – the story of a Nordic Romeo and Juliet, frustrated by their families' political strife. Victor Hugo's social conscience was still relatively undeveloped – he was not yet over-preoccupied with the social themes that would dominate his later work; above all, he sought to become a member of the French House of Lords in recognition of his literary gifts.

In 1821, Sophie Hugo died, and Victor started wooing Adèle again – to the Fouchers' considerable annoyance, for now *they* felt their handsome daughter could make a better match. His persistence was, however, rewarded; they were married a year later.

Hugo, the compulsive keeper of diaries, has left a record of his wedding-night that conflicts considerably with the idealised version he sought to perpetuate through Marius and Cosette in *Les Misérables*. Both he and Adèle were virgins: on their wedding-night, Hugo was later to brag, he made love to her no less than nine times. Adèle, ill-prepared for this kind of assault, reacted with the submissiveness of a nineteenth-century wife conscious of her sexual subordination, but her feelings for him were never to be the same again. Hugo seems to have had no awareness of his young bride's true state of mind.

A series of almost yearly pregnancies followed, but after a fifth child, Léopoldine, was born in 1830, Adèle Hugo, to her husband's considerable surprise and dismay, put an abrupt stop

Victor Hugo, aged eighteen

This is how *La Mode*, a French fashion magazine, saw Victor Hugo's wife, Adèle, in the early days of her husband's fame

to their sexual relations. In common with other nineteenth-century males (his feminist sympathies not yet manifest) Hugo believed that 'man has received from nature the key with which to wind up his wife every twenty-four hours' ('some women', he noted, 'light up like a match'), and never came to terms with his wife's decision. He was even more embittered when she began a discreet, lengthy liaison with his erstwhile friend Sainte-Beuve, a writer of surpassing ugliness.

Victor Hugo was now, at twenty-three, a literary celebrity, a member of the Legion of Honour (for services to literature) and the acknowledged leader of a 'new wave' of writers and poets. His royalist fervour was waning, his humanitarian concern for have-nots gradually coming to the fore, at complete odds with the reactionary regime of Charles X. Hugo's new play, *Marion Delorme*, a romantic tragedy, was banned by the censors, a ruling upheld by the King himself. And in 1829, a visit to Bicêtre prison turned Hugo, almost overnight, into an abolitionist; he wrote an essay on capital punishment (*Le dernier jour d'un condamné*). It was the first of many writings on prison life, torture and executions, topics that would obsess him all his life.

By 1830 he had become such a party-giver that his landlord asked him to leave: his guests made too much noise. That year Charles X was compelled to resign: his successor, Louis Philippe, a republican-minded monarch, a tolerant, good-natured liberal, was a great admirer of Victor Hugo and made him a peer.

These were Hugo's most glittering years. He had moved into a mansion on the Place Royale (now the Place des Vosges, and the Victor Hugo Museum in Paris). Crowds waited outside to catch a glimpse of the rich and famous on their way to his parties. Victor Hugo's fame, as a poet and successful dramatist, was like that of today's pop stars and, like them, he was pursued by attractive women. One of them, Juliette Drouet, became his mistress, secretary, slave and lifelong companion.

Born Julienne-Joséphine Gauvain, Juliette had been a teenage model posing nude for sculptors, an unmarried mother (at nineteen) and was packed off to a repertory company in Brussels as an aspiring actress. Back in Paris, where she ran up huge debts, paid for by a succession of rich lovers, she got a tiny part in one of Hugo's plays. She was pretty, graceful, had a quick, lively mind and was unabashedly sexual; Victor Hugo had never met anyone like her before. Their love affair – celebrated extravagantly in verse and prose by the prolific letter-writer and poet – began one carnival night and was the talk of the town.

Adèle Hugo was fully aware of the affair, for Victor Hugo now spent his nights with Juliette, returning home, his friends noted, 'only at mealtimes'. Juliette called him 'le grand Toto',

This portrait of Juliette Drouet by A.-Ch. Voillemot (1823-1893) reveals her sexuality and ethereal beauty. Though she aged prematurely and Hugo increasingly sought excitement elsewhere, Juliette remained his lifelong companion and some of her own love-letters to Victor Hugo were both touching and humorous. In a mock creditor's letter, scribbled in a restaurant after a meal with him, she acknowledged 'receipt from Mr Hugo of a great deal of love, a great deal of happiness and a great deal of devotion, which I hereby agree to repay on sight'. Conjugal fidelity, at the time, was, as a contemporary noted, 'essentially a bourgeois virtue', and his liaison was condoned by his wife, his friends, and King Louis Philippe himself.

Although he was now a successful writer, with an assured income, Victor Hugo was, nevertheless, careful with money, and Juliette was, at first, an expensive mistress. Hugo now supported two households, but balked at settling Juliette's mounting debts, paying her instead a miserly 1000 francs a month, part of which she spent on her lover's meals (he was inordinately fond of expensive food like truffles).

Hugo's physical passion soon began to wane (in her letters to him, Juliette complained he no longer made love to her with the same ardour or frequency) and Hugo started seeing other women behind her back. But he never broke with Juliette, who became a 'second wife' to him – protective, admiring, submissive, a 'back-street' figure sacrificing her entire life to his. Occasionally she rebelled, but Hugo's personality, fame and undeniable powers of seduction all conspired to keep her, as she once wrote, 'like a dog on a chain'. Furthermore, his fame as a playwright did not lead, as Juliette had hoped in the beginning, to a successful stage career for herself. Rival actresses, and Adèle Hugo herself, saw to that: for all Adèle's urging her husband 'not to deny yourself anything . . . I have no more need of pleasure . . . You poor old thing, who got married at twenty, I have no wish to have you bind your life to the old woman I have become', she nevertheless used her considerable influence with theatre directors to deny Juliette any parts in her husband's plays.

By 1841 Victor Hugo was not only a peer but a member of the French Academy, a literary giant whose motto was 'Ego Hugo'. His prodigious sexual appetite found an outlet in countless casual affairs with actresses and socialites. He still spent part of the year, however, with Juliette, who remained blissfully unaware of her lover's infidelity. It was while they were holidaying together in 1843 that Léopoldine, his newly-married youngest daughter, was drowned in a boating accident. Victor Hugo's grief at her death was heart-rending.

As a member of the French House of Lords, he was now a public figure and prolific speech-maker, still a Royalist, but an eloquent exponent of Louis Philippe's own liberal monarchical brand. France was embarking on decades of political turmoil, and Hugo was starting to become the champion of the underdog. His clashes with the law, at this stage of his life, however,

Victor Hugo during his exile in Belgium

were of another nature altogether: adultery was still a criminal offence, and when in 1845 a jealous husband complained to the police of his wife's infidelity, a police inspector caught her and Victor Hugo in *flagrante delicto*. While Hugo successfully claimed parliamentary immunity (seeing to it that nothing appeared in the Press), his companion, on the other hand, was carted off to jail, then to a convent, where she remained for six months.

In 1848, the timid, middle-class monarchy of Louis Philippe was overthrown, and Victor Hugo, adjusting to the change, became a prominent Republican Member of Parliament. He still spoke in favour of 'order, property and family', at heart still a middle-of-the-road Conservative, but the Paris barricades, the turmoil in the streets, and the bitter plight of the under-privileged, had left their mark, and he had already begun writing *Les Misérables*. The mob that had built barricades and run rampage through Paris had briefly occupied his house on the renamed Place des Vosges, using it as a workers' headquarters, but had not looted it. 'So many brave soldiers! and oh! those poor, misguided workers!' he wrote to Adèle.

As Charles Louis Napoleon, soon to become dictator, gathered power, Victor Hugo was briefly attracted to him, with visions of himself as the writer-politician who would eradicate social injustice, establish compulsory free education for all, and turn France into Europe's most 'advanced' nation. He expressed his views in the liberal daily, *L'événement*. Conservatives called him a turncoat. Hugo noted, in his diary, that 'with the help of meditation, by degrees, like many of my contemporaries, I came to embrace the ideas of my age and my country. In my obscure and limited person, I am a living proof of the truth and irresistible force which you [Conservatives] oppose.' He was becoming an authentic hero to the poor: at Balzac's funeral, in 1850, he was mobbed by thousands of working-class admirers.

Hugo was also facing domestic problems: in June 1851, out of spite, one of Hugo's mistresses, Léonie d'Aunet, sent Juliette Drouet a bundle of love letters Victor Hugo had been unwise enough to write to her. Juliette became distraught, threatening suicide, but her mood didn't last. Hugo was able to convince the prematurely aged and white-haired Juliette that she was still the only real love in his life, and when the crunch came, a few months later, she once more proved the strength of her attachment to him.

For in December 1851, Charles Louis Napoleon seized power in a classic *putsch* and proclaimed himself President. Hugo, now an acknowledged radical, and prominent intellectual leader of the French Republican Left, vigorously protested the illegal coup, though his many enemies claimed he had only turned against the new dictator because he had been refused the

Education Ministry portfolio. He now faced arrest, and a possible death penalty.

With the help of the faithful Juliette, Hugo fled to Brussels. Overnight, the millionaire writer and prominent politician became a near-pauper and an exile, his assets in jeopardy, his family dispersed. After a spell in Brussels, then one in London, he finally settled in the Channel Islands, after the contents of his Paris house were auctioned off for a ridiculously low sum.

In Jersey, whence he was expelled for making disparaging remarks about Queen Victoria for her cordial relations with Napoleon III, then in Guernsey, at Hauteville House, that huge, sombre mansion full of baroque furniture, Hugo became one of the world's earliest and most famous dissidents: refusing all offers of an amnesty from the man he had dubbed 'Napoleon the Small', he lived in patriarchal splendour, with his extended family – with Juliette Drouet in a small house near-by. Instead of actresses and socialites, there was now a steady stream of local girls, many of them housemaids, whom he coaxed into bed, carefully noting, in an easily decipherable code, his payments to them, and the nature of their sexual services. Adèle quickly tired of Hauteville House, spending more and more time in Paris.

It was only in 1860 that Victor Hugo resumed work on *Les Misérables*, which he had put aside after the 1848 revolution, when active involvement in politics reduced his literary output. In his Guernsey retreat, he worked fast and then left for Belgium, where he spent several months inserting the chapters on the battle of Waterloo, wandering over the battlefield, picking up spent bullets, even a ragged flag. Juliette Drouet wrecked her eyesight deciphering Hugo's spindly handwriting in order to provide his publishers with a fair copy.

Victor Hugo launched *Les Misérables* in Brussels in 1862 with the practised skill of the born media star. It became an instant literary phenomenon, making Hugo enormously rich once more. It was, however, a popular rather than a critical success: most French literary critics attacked it for its excessive sentimentality, and the authoritarian government of 'Napoleon the Small' banned the play based on the book.

Adèle Hugo died in 1868, and Victor Hugo accompanied her coffin only as far as the Franco-Belgian border – he still refused to return home. His family life was disintegrating: he quarrelled with his sons, and his surviving daughter, also called Adèle, ran off to Canada to be with a young British officer, Albert Pinson, whom she claimed she married, later pursuing him all the way to Barbados. She was already showing signs of mental instability and persecution mania that would eventually have tragic consequences. Victor Hugo, now a legendary figure, held court in Hauteville House, visited London and Brussels regularly, played with his grandchildren, and waited for France to get rid of Napoleon III.

Hauteville House, Guernsey

Victor Hugo in exile in Jersey, 1852

Hugo's self-portrait – 'Mr Victor in the Sun'

Victor Hugo, the father of
*Les Misérables*

In 1870, this finally happened. The Franco-Prussian war which the French dictator had confidently expected to win, led instead to a series of defeats and his country's collapse. Napoleon fled to Britain, and Hugo did something he had refused to do for twenty years: he took the train from Brussels, arriving at the Gare du Nord to a beleaguered, wartime Paris. The delirious welcome Hugo received from the Parisians repaid him, 'in one hour', he told them, 'for twenty years of exile'. But the city he returned to was on the brink of armed rebellion, and France perilously close to civil war.

Hugo was immediately elected Member of Parliament by the Parisians. He had become, not only a symbol of the left, but, through his writings, the incarnation of resistance to the invaders. More realistically, the government that succeeded Louis Napoleon, headed by Thiers, realised the hopelessness of France's military situation and sought peace at any price. In the new National Assembly, meeting not in rebellious Paris but in the safety of provincial Bordeaux, Victor Hugo spoke out against the humiliating terms of the armistice, which surrendered all of Alsace and part of Lorraine to Germany.

Like most of the Paris working-class population, Victor Hugo was a partisan of continued opposition at any price, of the kind of mass mobilisation against France's enemies that had occurred during the French Revolution. But this fighting spirit went hand in hand with revolutionary fervour: the radical theories of Blanqui and other French Socialists had had their effect. The French working class was in favour of total war against the German invaders, but only as part of a revolutionary upheaval bringing radical social and political change in its wake. France's government wanted neither a continuation of the war nor reforms of any kind. A head-on collision was inevitable, for to the leaders of the Paris 'Commune' the Conservative French government was as much the enemy of France as the German troops encircling Paris.

Victor Hugo was now an unabashed radical and an intellectual supporter of the notion embodied in the revolutionary Paris 'Commune', though he balked at the violence many of its leaders deemed necessary to bring it about. As an MP meeting in emergency session in Bordeaux, Hugo was, however, in a small minority. And though he spoke in favour of war, he also pleaded for the ultimate reconciliation of a Republican France and a Democratic Germany, a vision of a 'United States of Europe' few of his admirers shared or understood.

Hugo resigned, following a few months of frustrating failure and a campaign of personal insults against him. He now felt he would never be more than a maverick outsider in French politics. While Hugo was still in Bordeaux, his elder son, Charles, died suddenly of a brain haemorrhage and Victor Hugo brought him back to Paris to be buried in the family vault

'Victor Hugo sur son rocher' by
X.-A. Monchablon (1837-1907),
portraying the poet in exile

at the Père Lachaise cemetery. The cortège was mobbed by thousands of workers, in honour of Victor Hugo; he was still their popular, glamorous hero.

Ironically, his son's death meant Victor Hugo would be a distant spectator during the brief, bloody episode of the Paris 'Commune' uprising of May 1871. Charles's complicated inheritance problems compelled Hugo to move to Brussels to unravel them, and the Commune uprising began while he was still there. Wisely, he did not attempt to return, but he followed the tragic events avidly, though with increasing gloom and foreboding.

For the revolutionary workers were crushed, and the repression that followed was extremely brutal: tens of thousands were killed or executed on the spot, tens of thousands more were sentenced to death or deported. Hugo was appalled, not only by this savagery but by the Belgian government's refusal to accept any 'Communards' on the run as political exiles. His own home in Brussels, he wrote, would always be a haven for them.

Belgian and French 'Young Conservative' bullyboys surrounded Hugo's house, broke windows, shouted threats ('down with Jean Valjean'), and instead of dispersing the demonstrators, the Belgian police stood idly by; a few days later, the Belgian authorities expelled him as a 'threat to security'.

An exile once more, Hugo now settled in a tiny village, Vianden, in Luxembourg, and after the turmoil caused by the Commune and its brutal aftermath had receded he returned to Paris, only briefly at first, spending two years in voluntary exile in Hauteville House. He constantly campaigned for a full amnesty for the 'Commune' prisoners and exiles, and in 1873 wrote *Quatre-Vingt-Treize*, an historical novel set in the darkest days of the French revolutionary 'terror' of 1793. The 'terror' he meant to stigmatise, of course, was that of post-Commune France.

When he did finally return to Paris, passions had cooled, and Republican France, for the first time, started treating him with the respect he knew he deserved. He was appointed to the Upper House, the Senate, in 1875, and immediately resumed his campaign for an amnesty for the 'Communards', and for free, compulsory education for all.

As the grand old man of French letters, Victor Hugo was now a symbol of the strife that had led to so much cruelty and bloodshed. On the avenue d'Eylau (now the avenue Victor-Hugo) he became a living legend, a monument, one of the marvels of France to be visited along with the Louvre and Chartres Cathedral. His plays were revived and performed to packed houses, and he was the coveted guest of honour at every major literary or theatrical event. To his intense satisfaction, the amnesty and education bills he had been advocating for years were finally passed. He became the Dean of the French Academy, and of the Senate.

His extraordinary sexual powers never flagged, as his secret notebooks show, and the faithful Juliette Drouet fought a losing battle, intercepting some letters, turning away would-be mistresses and begging Victor Hugo, in notes both witty and melancholic, 'not to endanger your health in this way'. Once more Hugo's was a glittering life, an unbroken succession of banquets, Senate debates, literary gatherings and other official functions, with himself the central attraction.

Behind this façade lurked the tragedy of his daughter Adèle: back from Barbados, and in a nursing home at Saint-Mandé, near Paris, she was clearly insane, a paranoid schizophrenic who would never again be able to live a normal life. Every time Hugo went to see her, he returned depressed and filled with thoughts of death. As his secret diaries show, however, he did – broken-hearted as he was at his daughter Adèle's breakdown – seduce the maid from the West Indies who accompanied her back to France, noting, 'my first black!' With the exception of Adèle (who died in 1915), Hugo outlived all his children; François-Victor died of tuberculosis in 1873.

Victor Hugo, by Auguste Rodin (1840-1917)

The French government and the city of Paris celebrated Victor Hugo's eightieth birthday with an extraordinary series of pageants and processions, filling the avenue d'Eylau with banks of flowers, renaming part of it 'avenue Victor-Hugo'. Over several days, hundreds of thousands of people paraded in front of his house. They had come from all over France, and from as far away as Canada and California. No such tribute had ever been paid to a French writer before. Shortly afterwards, Juliette Drouet died of cancer, and Victor Hugo, showing signs of frailty at last, was too ill to go to her funeral.

In 1885, not long after making yet another public appearance with the cast of one of his plays, Victor Hugo caught a chill, dying of pleurisy a few days later. He had requested burial in a pauper's coffin, and – while stating in his will his belief in God – requested that no formal religious service be held.

What happened in the last week of May 1885 has been the subject of considerable scrutiny by historians, sociologists and political analysts alike ever since: the government debated whether to abide by Victor Hugo's wishes, or give him a State funeral. Over the objections of the extreme left (for whom Hugo, for all his humanitarianism, remained a 'bourgeois' traitor to the revolution) and the extreme Catholic right, who still regarded him as a dangerous rebel heretic, it was finally decided that Hugo's remains would lie in state for twenty-four hours in a plain coffin under the Arc de Triomphe and would then be taken, in an officially attended procession, to the Panthéon, where France's greatest men and women are buried.

All those who witnessed the proceedings were amazed by the

extraordinary fervour and enthusiasm that preceded the burial: huge crowds gathered at the Arc de Triomphe several days in advance of the vigil. The streets and gardens adjoining the Champs Élysées were packed with crowds of people of every class and condition: prostitutes and priests, intellectuals and shopkeepers, respectable families and hoodlums from Pigalle all mingled in paying this last homage to Victor Hugo. As writer witnesses like Edmond Goncourt, Maurice Barrès and the young Romain Rolland all recalled later, this was no sombre, mournful occasion. Instead, a party atmosphere prevailed, reminiscent of a fairground celebration, with much eating, drinking, dancing and lovemaking in the shrubbery and under the trees in the public gardens on either side of the Champs Élysées, to such an extent that one writer claimed the Paris birth-rate must have shot up nine months later. And when, on 1 June 1885, the funeral march started – headed by the French government, and including every conceivable French association of note – it was followed by several million ordinary French men, women and children. The procession from the Étoile to the Panthéon on the Left Bank took most of the day. Shops, restaurants, cafés and brothels were closed. Foreigners present couldn't believe their eyes. Famous writers and politicians fought to be allowed to take part in the official cortège, and to say a few words over the coffin. Victor Hugo's funeral oration – read by the French Prime Minister, Henri Brisson – reflected the mood of the nation and of the world. 'What man of our time is not indebted to him?' he asked. 'Democracy everywhere laments his passing.'

No Paris event before or since Victor Hugo's funeral – not even de Gaulle's famous walk down the Champs Élysées after the liberation of Paris, in 1944 – has ever attracted such crowds. The joyful mood of the participants, the absence of social barriers, the good-tempered, celebratory nature of the crowds camping around the Arc de Triomphe and the Champs Élysées came as a total surprise to the authorities and journalists alike.

The most likely explanation is that, in paying their final respects to Victor Hugo, the French people were celebrating the end of an era and of a century marked by wars of conquest, civil conflicts, brutally repressed insurrections and social injustice. In their minds, Victor Hugo, through his writings, ideals and personal life style, was the embodiment of a new, democratic spirit at large, not just in France, but throughout the modern world. The demons of Napoleon the Great and Napoleon 'the Small' had been exorcised at last.

Victor Hugo's passing also marked, however, the beginning of a new, more egalitarian, more hopeful Europe: Hugo's humane pantheism, his optimistic vision of the future, his belief in the triumph of good over evil and in the virtues of the

Victor Hugo's catafalque under the Arc de Triomphe, Paris, 1885

common people, were inspiring a deeply emotional, joyful response. After so much strife, so much bloodshed and cruelty, the mourners were at last acclaiming a hero whose lifelong message had been an emotional cry for tolerance and non-violence. This is the same message of hope that 'Les Misérables', the musical, conveys, in its unforgettable finale:

> Do you hear the people sing
> Lost in the valley of the night?
> It is the music of a people
> Who are climbing to the light.
> For the wretched of the earth
> There is a flame that never dies.
> Even the darkest night will end
> And the sun will rise.
> Is there a world you long to see?
> Do you hear the people sing?
> Say, do you hear the distant drums?
> It is the future that they bring
> When tomorrow comes!

This photograph of Victor Hugo on his death-bed was taken by French caricaturist and photographer, Nadar (1820-1910), on 24 May 1885

That universal appeal explains why, at the end of *Les Misérables*, audiences all over the world leave the theatre both uplifted and in tears.

# Victor Hugo
## and the Making of
# Les Misérables

For all his prodigious story-telling gifts and imaginative powers, Victor Hugo's *Les Misérables* is full of autobiographical allusions and only slightly transposed personal reminiscences.

There was no single model for any of its huge cast of characters, with the exception of the saintly Bishop of Digne, Charles-François-Bienvenu Myriel, the instrument of Jean Valjean's conversion, who was based on Monseigneur Miollis, a real-life character who really had been Bishop of Digne. But at almost every turn, Hugo drew on his own past, and on his prodigious visual memory. The very genesis of the book, in its original form (for like its title, originally *Misères*, then *La Misère*, it went through as many incarnations as the name of its principal hero, originally called Jean Tréjean), was a chance encounter, observed by Hugo on the rue de Tournon in 1845 and described by him in his diary as follows:

I was on my way to the House of Lords. It was a beautiful, sunny but cold day . . . Along the rue de Tournon came a man escorted by two soldiers. He was fair-haired, pale, thin, haggard-looking; about thirty, in coarse cotton trousers, bare scratched feet in wooden clogs, with bloody strips of cloth around the ankles instead of socks; a short shirt, stained with mud at the back, proof that he usually slept in the open air; bare-headed, spiky hair. Under his arm was a loaf of bread. The small crowd around him said he had stolen the loaf and that was why he had been arrested. He was outside the Gendarmerie barracks: one of the soldiers went inside, the other stayed outside with the man.

A vehicle drew up outside the Gendarmerie gates. It was a ducal carriage with crowns on the twin lamps, an armorial inscription on the doors, two bays in front, two gaitered, livery footmen at the back. The windows were closed, but one could catch a glimpse of the golden-point damask upholstery inside.

The man was staring inside the carriage, and I followed his gaze. Inside was a young woman in a black velvet dress and a pink hat, fair, fresh-faced, dazzlingly beautiful, merrily playing with a charming burbling, sixteen-month-old child, half hidden under ribbons, embroidery and furs.

She was not aware of the awesomely frightening man's stare.

I gave the matter some thought.

This was no longer a man, but the spectre of misery, the ghostly forewarning, in full light of day, in the sunshine, of a revolution still

Fantine sells her hair

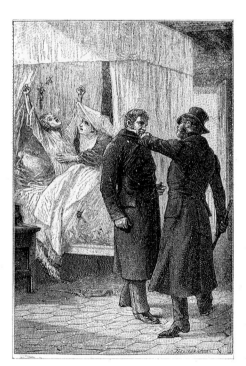

The death of Fantine

This painting of Jean Valjean in the first edition of *Les Misérables*, made it possible for Colm Wilkinson to keep the beard which Trevor Nunn had initially wanted him to shave off for the musical

plunged in the shadows of darkness, but emerging from them. In earlier times the wretched frayed with the wealthy, this wraith met that glory; but they didn't stare: they went their separate ways. This could have gone on for a long, long time. But from the moment he became aware of her existence, while she remained unaware of his, a catastrophe was inevitable.

[Victor Hugo: *Choses Vues*, vol. 2, pp 333/4]

Victor Hugo had already started preliminary work on *La Misère* but there can be no doubt that the incident on the rue de Tournon was a key, turning Hugo's saga of working-class despair into the spiritual adventure of the 'reborn' Jean Valjean, giving it a central character. It is also certain that Hugo was inspired by his frequent visits to French gaols: as a peer, he had permanent 'visitor privileges' to study and inspect the French prison system. After one of his visits, long before 'inventing' Valjean, Hugo wrote:

The sentenced man had to become a frightening figure; chained, he had to inspire fear, free he was meant to provoke horror. The ticket-of-leave man was a kind of demon deliberately fashioned by the law.

Incorporated in *Les Misérables* were memories of all kinds from Hugo's own childhood, of sights and smells, moods, tantrums and childish fears. Young Marius Pontmercy *was* young Hugo in almost every respect – both of them aristocrats, with military family antecedents. Like Hugo in his early days, Marius 'was a Royalist, fanatical and austere, fiery and cold, noble, generous, proud, religious, exalted, dignified to the point of harshness, pure to the extent of savagery'. Marius' student poverty mirrored young Hugo's own. So did his possessive jealousy: Marius warned Cosette against lifting her skirts when crossing puddles, because he didn't want her to display her ankles to all and sundry. Young Hugo similarly chided his teenage sweetheart Adèle for doing just that. From the pavement, through an open window, Marius, like Hugo, during those wretched years when his mother put a stop to his love affair with Adèle, saw Cosette dancing with someone else at a party, and was, like him, consumed with jealousy and hopeless grief.

In *Les Misérables* is the grim aphorism: 'perfect happiness does not laugh. Utter grief does not cry.' The real-life Victor Hugo hated the good-natured banter and jollity that was a feature of his own wedding: the stern, prim young man felt this was a solemn occasion. But the romantic description of Marius' first night of love with Cosette in *Les Misérables*, was, in fact, the juxtaposition of two memories: that of Hugo's actual wedding-night with Adèle, as he later idealised it, and of his first night with Juliette Drouet, when they made love to the distant sound of the carnival in the streets below.

*Les Misérables* is the story of a city almost as much as that of

Cosette or Jean Valjean. Again and again, Hugo introduces glimpses of the Paris he had known as a child. Much of it only existed in his imagination, for many of the landmarks he cherished had been pulled down as a result of Baron Haussmann's officially encouraged rebuilding spree, and in a brief aside to his readers, Hugo obliquely referred to his Guernsey exile, noting that he had had no recent opportunity of vouching for the accuracy of the city he described. He included vignettes of his early family life: Jean Valjean and Cosette walked hand in hand in Montfermeil just as Hugo had walked with his own favourite daughter, Léopoldine.

Hugo also used the bestselling novelist's trick of mixing trivial everyday fact with fiction – referring to real-life murder cases that had been of interest to Parisians, mentioning the streets where they had occurred, as Valjean or Marius crossed and recrossed these landmarks in Hugo's beloved Paris. These references had nothing to do with the narrative, but unlike the immensely long section on the battle of Waterloo they were not literary red herrings: they gave the itineraries of Valjean, Marius and others unique journalistic veracity.

Hugo also drew on the early experiences of those close to him: Cosette's childhood traumas and convent education, as described in *Les Misérables*, owed a lot to Juliette Drouet's reminiscences and pillow-talk; Montreuil-sur-Mer, where Jean Valjean, his past concealed, became the respectable business-man and mayor, was not chosen at random: Hugo had spent several vacations there, and knew it well. As Hugo's biographer, Hubert Juin, wrote, 'When Hugo travels, he creates'. Jean Valjean's dreams were Hugo's, too, and even the framed print on the Thénardier bedroom wall was based on a picture similar to one Hugo remembered from his own childhood.

One episode in *Les Misérables* (in both the book and the musical) is of crucial dramatic importance: Fantine's arrest by Javert for striking a young aristocrat after the snowball scene. The incident was drawn from real life, with almost no frills or changes, the only difference being that while the actual event took place in Paris, Hugo's version in *Les Misérables* happened in Montreuil-sur-Mer.

Here is Hugo's diary for 9 January 1841, telling the story as it occurred. Because he dictated this entry to Adèle, it is written in the third person. He had been to a dinner party given in his honour a few days after his third (and successful) attempt to be elected to the French Academy:

Victor Hugo left quite early, about nine p.m. It was snowing heavily. He was wearing his thin-soled shoes, and knew it would be impossible to return home on foot. He walked down the rue Taitbout, because he knew that's where cabs waited. There were none.

He was standing there, when he saw a young man, in sharp,

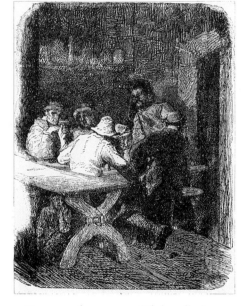

Taproom loungers at Thénardier's

Scenes from *Les Misérables* became popular themes for nineteenth-century painters. This painting by Jean Geoffroy (1853-1924) was one of many depicting Valjean and Cosette's first meeting

expensive clothes, pick up a handful of snow and shove it down the back of a streetwalker who was standing on the corner, wearing a décolleté dress.

She let out a shriek, turned on the dandy and hit him. The man retaliated, so did she, the battle escalated to such an extent that the police arrived.

They grabbed the girl; they didn't touch the man.

When they laid hands on her, the poor girl fought them. Once they had a good hold on her, she displayed the deepest grief.

While the two cops were forcemarching her along, each holding her by the arm, she was shouting: 'I swear, I didn't do any harm, *he* did me harm. I'm not guilty; let me go, I beg you. I didn't do anything wrong, I'm not guilty, I swear, I swear.'

The cops weren't listening. They just said: 'Get a move on. You'll get six months for this . . .'

They took her to the police station behind the Opéra.

V.H., interested in the poor girl despite himself, followed, part of the crowd that always gathers in such circumstances.

He thought of going inside, and of giving evidence in the girl's favour. But he knew he was well known, that the papers had mentioned him only a couple of days previously, and that to get involved would provoke all sorts of innuendoes. In short, he decided against it.

The girl was waiting in a room giving onto the street. He could see what was going on through the windows. He saw her rolling on the ground in despair, tearing her hair. Compassion grew, he began to have second thoughts, and as a result walked into the police station.

A clerk sitting at a candle-lit desk said gruffly, 'What do you want, Sir?'

'I was a witness to what occurred. I wish to testify in favour of this woman.'

At these words, the girl looked at V.H., mute with astonishment, as though shocked.

'Sir, such a testimony, more or less biased, would be of no value whatsoever. She is guilty of a street offence, she has a beaten a gentleman. She'll get six months.'

The girl started crying again and rolling about on the floor. Other prostitutes were trying to calm her down. 'We'll bring you clean underthings,' they said. 'Here, take this,' and they gave her sweets and money.

'Sir,' said V.H., 'when you know who I am you will, perhaps, change your tone and language and maybe you will listen to me.'

'And pray who are you, Sir?'

V.H. saw no reason to hold the information back. He declared his identity. The police station chief apologised profusely, became as polite and as deferent as he had been arrogant, and asked him to take a seat.

V.H. described how he had seen, with his own eyes, the 'gentleman' take a handful of snow and stuff it down the girl's back; how she, not even knowing who he was, had let out a sharp cry, had then turned on

The episode leading to Fantine's meeting with Valjean was based on a real-life incident witnessed by Hugo. This illustration appeared in the first edition of Hugo's diaries, *Choses Vues*

the 'gentleman', but in self-defence; how, apart from the indignity involved, the bitter cold and the snow down her back could do her great harm; how – rather than prevent this miserable woman, who perhaps had a mother or an infant child to look after, from exercising her wretched profession – it was the man who should have been charged and arrested, not her.

As he said all this, the girl's surprise was more and more evident, she looked radiant. 'How good the gentleman is,' she said. 'You know, I'd never seen 'im before, I swear I don't even know 'im.'

[Victor Hugo: *Choses Vues*, vol. 2, pp 204–8]

Victor Hugo agreed to sign his statement, and the girl was freed. She kept saying, 'How good the gentleman is, my God, how good!' As Hugo added, somewhat complacently, 'these unfortunate women are not only astonished and grateful when one is compassionate towards them: they react in the same way when one is fair to them.'

[Victor Hugo: *Choses Vues*, vol. 2, p 208]

When Hugo started writing *Les Misérables* he was a middle-of-the-road Conservative, a peer, one of the best-known figures on the French social scene, a dazzlingly successful poet and playwright courted by 'le tout Paris'. By 1861, when he concluded the book, after a twelve-year break, he had been in exile for over ten years, had moved steadily to the left ever since the December 1851 *putsch*, and had become a genuine radical. The barricades he described in *Les Misérables* assumed, in retrospect, a mythic quality which they had not had in 1832, when he had witnessed them: in his diary, he noted them only briefly at the time, as 'madness drowned in blood'. Though Hugo sympathised to some extent with the student and working-class minority that rioted during the funeral of General Lamarque, he was – when these riots occurred – by no means a Republican; in the troubled, violent history of nineteenth-century France, the 1832 riots were in fact very minor happenings. But, because the historical backdrop to *Les Misérables* spanned the Napoleonic era as well as the later, royalist period, he was compelled to use the comparatively unimportant Lamarque barricades for the dénouement of his saga. The 1848 'revolution' and the disturbances that took place at the time of Napoleon III's initial 1851 *putsch*, had been far more dramatic, but he could not include these in *Les Misérables* for several reasons: the 1851 *putsch* would have thrown the chronology out of kilter, for he would have had to have added twenty years to the lives of his characters. As for the barricades of the 1848 'revolution', which had been on a far greater scale, Hugo faced a personal problem – he had intervened politically then, urging Parisians to accept a Regency, and had been shouted down by the mob. This precluded him from writing about them with the kind of fervour and enthusiasm he could conjure up for the

Little Gavroche

A gifted caricaturist, Hugo drew this picture of Gavroche to keep the character in his mind's eye as he wrote *Les Misérables*

1832 barricades. Ironically, the events he described so dramatically would become appallingly real during the Paris Commune which took place nine years *after Les Misérables* was
published.

Since the events described in *Les Misérables* occurred, another
change had overtaken Victor Hugo: for all his frenzied sexual
drive, he had become a deeply religious non-conformist, who
believed that all organised religions, however well-intentioned,
had failed to bring the reality of God into the hearts and minds
of mankind. 'All religions must be destroyed in order to rebuild
God,' he wrote in 1860. 'By this I mean: rebuild Him within
the human spirit (*le reconstruire dans l'homme*).' 'This is a
religious book,' he wrote in a preface to *Les Misérables* that
remained unpublished, at his own request.

It wasn't easy for Hugo to return to the manuscript of *Les
Misérables* after such a long interruption, but from 1860 he
worked on it day and night, and in 1861 lugged the huge
manuscript with him in a waterproof bag from Guernsey to
Weymouth to Brussels, revising and adding to it as he travelled.
On 30 June 1861, he wrote: 'This morning, at 8.30 a.m., I
finished "Les Misérables", on the site of the battle of Waterloo
and in the month of Waterloo . . . I am in no hurry to publish.'

Considerable revisions followed, lasting almost a year. 'I
must inspect the monster from head to foot', he wrote. 'This is a
leviathan I am about to ship out to sea.' For all his radicalism, he
remained an extraordinarily shrewd businessman where publishers were concerned. There had been considerable specula-
tion in the French and Belgian Press about the nature and
content of *Les Misérables*, and Hugo whetted the journalists'
appetites without giving anything away, beyond the cryptic
phrase, in a Brussels interview: 'Dante described hell in after-
life whereas I have described hell on earth.'

Well aware of his book's potential, Victor Hugo asked his
former publisher, Hetzel, for a 300,000 franc royalty in return
for a twelve-year publishing franchise. Hetzel was not able to
raise such a large sum. Albert Lacroix, a Brussels-based publisher and printer, was. Hugo drove a hard bargain: no pre-
publication extracts and no detailed summary of the book's
contents to be released to the Press. The press release, Hugo
wrote to Lacroix, 'should concentrate on "Notre-Dame de
Paris" [his earlier novel, featuring the saintly hunchback,
Quasimodo]. After the Middle Ages, modern times: that
should be the theme . . . What Victor H. did for the Gothic
world in "Notre-Dame de Paris", he accomplishes for the
modern world in "Les Misérables". These two books will be like
two mirrors reflecting humankind.' On 30 March 1862, the
first part of *Les Misérables*, 'Fantine', came off Lacroix's presses.
Proof-reading took several weeks, and the 'Fantine' and
'Marius' volumes finally went on sale in May 1862.

*Les Misérables* was not just a bestseller: in the entire history of publishing, there had been nothing to compare with the excitement it generated. The initial publication of *Les Misérables* became a media event. In the workshops where it was printed, workers clubbed together, each contributing twenty sous to a twelve-franc 'kitty'; a name was then pulled out of a hat, and the prize was a copy of *Les Misérables*. Advertisements all over Paris proclaimed the imminent arrival of *Les Misérables*, its main characters – Cosette, Fantine, Marius, Jean Valjean – illustrated in giant sketched portraits.

Bookshop owners, commissionaires with horsedrawn vehicles and delivery-boys pushing carts and barrows literally fought for copies of *Les Misérables* the day the Paris printing-shop, Pagnerre, finally began distribution. The frenzied queues were reminiscent of the long lines outside bakers' shops during severe bread shortages. Huge traffic jams developed as hundreds of people waited their turn to cart off their quota of the 48,000 copies put on sale that day.

Éponine finds Marius

Like the musical, over a hundred years later, Hugo's *Les Misérables* was, initially, a popular, rather than a critical success: 'All the reviews', Hugo noted, 'are reactionary and more or less hostile.' Georges Sand, who read the book in proof form, felt 'there was too much Christianity in it'. Hugo's old friend Théophile Gautier deliberately ignored *Les Misérables* in his literary column in *Le Moniteur*. Hugo expected adverse responses from the 'Catholic, reactionary and Bonapartist Press' but was shocked by the lukewarm review written by an old friend in *Le Siècle*, a liberal daily. Even Lamartine, in his 'Reflections on a Masterpiece, Or the Perils of Being a Genius' wrote that 'this is a dangerous book'. The effect of the Lamartine piece, Hugo noted, was 'like that of being pecked by a swan'. His erstwhile crony, Sainte-Beuve, now a bitter, vindictive enemy, wrote in his diary: '"Les Misérables" is everywhere, proof that the public's taste is really sick.' He didn't review it either. *La France* and the *Catholic World Review* spread the rumour that Hugo had deliberately delayed bringing the book out to wait for the most financially propitious moment. Charles Baudelaire, whom Hugo much admired, wrote him an approving letter, and then boasted of his hypocrisy to his mother: 'This is a vile and inept book', he told her.

The critics' opinions, however, had no effect whatsoever on public interest: sales were enormous, and the initial French-language publishing success was duplicated all over the world as soon as the book became available in translation. In a letter to his Italian publisher, Hugo wrote: 'You are right, Sir, when you say that "Les Misérables" is written for a universal audience. I don't know whether it will be read by everyone, but it is meant for everyone. It addresses England as well as Spain, Italy as well as France, Germany as well as Ireland, the republics that

*Overleaf:* Scenes from the play, *Les Misérables*, at the Théâtre de la Porte Saint-Martin

THEATRE DE

Types — I. Jean Valjean (M. Dumaine). — II. L'évêque Myriel (M. Lacressonnière). — III. Cosette (petite Daubray). — IV. Fantine (
(Mmes Morin et Berty). — IX. Thénardier (M. Vanoy). — X. La Thénardier (Mme Bardy). — Tableaux : 1. Retour de Jean Valjean,
7. M. Madeleine venant dire au tribunal d'Arras qu'il est Jean Valjean. — 8. Arrestation

harbour slaves as well as empires that have serfs. Social problems go beyond frontiers. Humankind's wounds, those huge sores that litter the world, do not stop at the blue and red lines drawn on maps. Wherever men go in ignorance or despair, wherever women sell themselves for bread, wherever children lack a book to learn from or a warm hearth, "Les Misérables" knocks at the door and says: "open up, I am here for you".' To this end Hugo urged his publisher to bring out a cheap version, in small print, to make it available to ordinary people.

Victor Hugo's message was spreading all over the world, but the campaign against him was only just beginning: the conservative *Les débats* claimed that *Les Misérables* 'is more dangerous than a socialist tract'; the *Constitutionnel* wrote that if the book's logic was admitted, 'no part of the social order would remain standing'; a theatrical version of *Les Misérables*, written by Hugo's son Charles, was banned in France, opening instead in Brussels; and in 1864, the Vatican included *Les Misérables* on its list of banned books (where it remained for several years).

Since then *Les Misérables* has been included on the school curriculum in many countries, not all of them French-speaking, and has been translated into almost every language. After the Bible, it is probably one of the world's bestselling books.

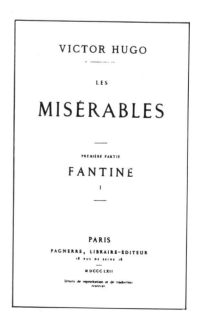

# Movers and Shakers

In his will, Victor Hugo instructed his heirs not to allow any of his poems to be set to music. He said nothing, however, about his novels. Several nineteenth-century composers, Puccini among them, toyed with the notion of turning *Les Misérables* into an opera, but it was to take 120 years for Hugo's masterpiece to be transformed into musical theatre, itself almost as famous as the original epic bestseller. But not everyone who sees the musical will have read the book, and the inevitable question is: how much of it had to be left out to produce a three-hour musical?

The answer is: surprisingly little. There are book-length digressions within Hugo's novel – essays on religion, Napoleon, Waterloo, French politics in the first half of the nineteenth century and French slang. At best, these are masterly, but some are self-indulgent, gratuitous displays of erudition.

The musical *Les Misérables* condenses some of the action, speeding up the plot: in the book, for instance, Valjean, as 'Monsieur Madeleine', the Mayor of Montreuil, surrenders to Javert, and goes back to jail. As a lifetime convict in the infamous Toulon 'bagne', Valjean reveals his heroic, self-sacrificial nature by saving the life of a drowning sailor. He escapes in the process, and is offically reported drowned. It is only at this stage – in the book – that he rescues Cosette from the Thénardiers, and takes her to Paris.

In the course of Valjean's lengthy stay in Paris, Victor Hugo uses dramatic devices to weave the Valjean, Javert, Thénardier and Marius stories into a whole which, with a lesser novelist, would strain the reader's credulity. For instance, the man who finds a hiding-place for Valjean inside the Petit-Picpus convent is none other than Fauchelevent, the carter whose life Valjean saved in Montreuil. Other coincidences follow thick and fast.

It transpires that it was Thénardier who tended Colonel Pontmercy, Marius's father, as he lay wounded on the battle-field of Waterloo so that the heroic colonel believed, to his dying day, that Thénardier saved his life. In fact, Thénardier was merely trying to rob what he thought was a corpse. In a posthumous message to his son, Marius, the colonel enjoins him to seek out Thénardier and reward him. Why he does not do this himself in his own lifetime remains unexplained.

Thénardier, it turns out, is Gavroche's father. Like Jean-Jacques Rousseau, he abandoned his baby at birth, and Gavroche never finds out who his father is. But a further, even

Alain Boublil and Claude-Michel Schönberg

Cameron Mackintosh

more improbable coincidence takes up much of the second volume of *Les Misérables*: young Marius Pontmercy, by now a fervent Bonapartist, has cut himself off from his wealthy family and is living in squalor in a Paris boarding-house. His next-door neighbour is none other than Thénardier. The inn having gone out of business, the Thénardiers have moved to Paris, where the villainous ex-innkeeper, now masquerading under various aliases, has become a small-time criminal, specialising in blackmail and confidence tricks.

In one of his scams, Thénardier poses as a down-and-out actor and Valjean, ever the soft touch, gives him money and clothing. But Thénardier (who fails to recognise the now older Valjean) believes him to be a fabulously wealthy old eccentric, and, thinking Cosette is Valjean's daughter, plans to kidnap her and hold her to ransom. Strangely, Valjean doesn't recognise Thénardier either. The kidnap plan goes wrong when Marius overhears part of Thénardier's conversation with his family, and goes to the nearest police station to prevent anything untoward happening to the young woman with whom he is already secretly in love. The inspector Marius talks to is none other than Javert. By the time the latter raids the boarding-house, Valjean is being held prisoner by Thénardier and his gang. Javert promptly arrests them. He does not, however, recognise Valjean, who, spotting Javert, wisely decamps through the window. French justice, so harsh on Valjean, is singularly lenient as far as the Thénardiers are concerned, for they are soon released and back in business.

On stage, such flimsy, implausible melodrama would have been too far-fetched; wisely, none of it is included in the musical *Les Misérables* which constitutes a leaner, more credible version of Hugo's plot, and is far stronger as narrative drama.

The teams that labour over the 'Les Mis' productions around the world today add up to several thousand people, but *Les Misérables*, the musical, would not have happened without the coming together of three people: Claude-Michel Schönberg, the composer; Alain Boublil, the lyricist who co-authored 'Les Mis'; and Cameron Mackintosh, who produced the English-language version premièred in 1985 and since seen, in half a dozen languages, all over the world.

## Alain Boublil and Claude-Michel Schönberg

Tunis-born Boublil did not have a musical background (his father owned a shoe shop) but he nevertheless developed a passion for American musicals although he didn't actually see any on stage until he went to Paris as a student of the Institute of Higher Commercial Studies (HEC). He recalls attending the

Paris première of *West Side Story* in 1959 (a friend of his father had given him a ticket) with a great sense of wonder. 'I came out of there saying to myself: "I can do that, I know I can",' he says. But the success of *Les Misérables* was preceded by a long, and often frustrating, apprenticeship.

Distantly related to the twentieth-century Austrian-born composer, Claude-Michel Schönberg was born in Vannes, Brittany, in 1941, the son of an organ repairer and piano tuner who emigrated from his native Hungary in the 1930s. From infancy, Schönberg lived in a highly musical environment. 'My father had a large collection of classical records,' he says. 'They were, of course, old 78s. Our "Madame Butterfly" was on thirty sides.' His first visit to the Paris Opéra, he recalls, was at the age of six. 'Other children give their mothers presents on their birthdays,' he says. 'I used to compose songs for her.' Musically self-taught, Schönberg was a fledgling artistic director for Pathé-Marconi records in Paris when he met Alain Boublil, with whom he has worked for the last twenty years.

Instead of joining a bank or major corporation, like most HEC graduates, Boublil took a job with the French radio station, Europe Numéro Un, acting briefly as their pop records programmer and writing song lyrics on the side. He then joined a record company himself, as a producer, marrying Françoise Pourcel, the daughter of a well-known orchestra leader and recording artist; Schönberg was Franck Pourcel's record producer.

From their first encounter, Boublil and Schönberg discovered they had in common a passion for musicals and opera, but initially they went their separate ways: Boublil set up his own publishing company, also writing songs for others while Schönberg pursued his career as a record producer.

Then in 1973, came a moment that changed the course of Boublil's life. He was invited to the première of *Jesus Christ Superstar* in New York. It was, he recalls, an overwhelming experience. The Lloyd Webber-Rice musical represented an art form Boublil had instinctively been drawn to, without ever believing it could be realised in a world increasingly dominated by pop and disco music: an all-sung musical with an historical theme, mixing the tradition of Italian opera with contemporary musical and literary styles. After the performance, he walked the Manhattan streets in a daze, unable to sleep. As Boublil recalls, he felt an overwhelming compulsion to keep walking until he'd thought of a suitable theme for a rock opera that might compare in scope and emotional intensity with the subject matter of *Jesus Christ Superstar*. Inspiration came at dawn: why not deal with the single most important event in French history – the French Revolution?

Back in Paris he put forward this 'crazy project' to his co-writer friend, Jean-Max Rivière, and composers Raymond

*Overleaf*: 'Look Down', London

Jeannot and Claude-Michel Schönberg, all of whom enthusiastically endorsed it. The result was the show, *La Revolution
Française*. It became a bestselling record and was subsequently
staged for a solid season at the Palais des Sports with Schönberg
himself singing the part of Louis XVI.

A series of abortive projects followed. Then, some years later,
while both Boublil and Schönberg were looking for a suitable
theme for a new musical, Boublil saw a revival of the British
musical *Oliver!* in London. The producer was a young man
called Cameron Mackintosh, but this meant nothing to him at
the time. What mattered was an idea – almost a revelation –
that came to Boublil as he watched the story unfold. 'As soon as
the Artful Dodger came on stage,' says Boublil, 'Gavroche came
to mind. It was like a blow to the solar plexus. I started seeing all
the characters of Victor Hugo's "Les Misérables" – Valjean,
Javert, Gavroche, Cosette, Marius and Éponine – in my mind's
eye, laughing, crying and singing on stage.' He broached the
subject to Schönberg who said, 'Let's do it,' and immediately
left his record-company job to work full time on the project.

'It was lèse-majesté on our part,' says Boublil, 'a monumental, monstrous piece of cheek to dare compress the world-
famous epic novel into a piece of musical theatre. We were
scared to tamper with it in any way. In any case we knew we had
to kick the idea around for weeks if not months, talking about
it, picking holes in it, discussing the book aimlessly but with an
ultimate purpose, to see whether it would work as a musical or
not, and whether the gods would be on our side.'

The first step in writing a sung-through, French-language
version of *Les Misérables*, says Boublil, was simply to read the
book again, with no thought of either words or music. That
first essential stage, both men agree, was necessary to establish
the story line, the characters and the climaxes. 'We told each
other the story visually,' says Schönberg, 'asking each other,
"What is actually happening on stage?" "What are the characters saying to each other?" "What are they trying to convey?"
"What is the audience absorbing, or learning?" The question
uppermost in our minds was always: what is the spectator's
reaction to all this, at any given moment?' They were discovering, for themselves, the rules inherent in the writing of musical
theatre, drawing up a detailed, descriptive treatment of the
music and lyrics to come, summing up the moods of each
succeeding scene.

Only once this initial process was complete did Schönberg
start work on the music. 'I tackled it chronologically,' he says,
'working eight hours a day. When writing a short song, one can
wait for inspiration to come. With something as long as musical
theatre, one has to slog away. There are times when you get
stuck. Two weeks can go by without producing a decent bar of
music.'

As was his habit, Schönberg taped everything as he went along. When he had a workable musical sequence, he played it through to Boublil on the piano. Boublil then took the tapes, and went away to work on a first draft of the libretto on his own. When *that* stage was complete, they came together again. 'Of course, we tore out whole chunks of text and music,' says Schönberg. 'What was important was to have something on paper, and on tape, that we could work on together. We knew that however hard we worked, what we would end up with would only be an initial draft, and that a long, polishing process lay ahead.' Boublil describes this as a constant cross-questioning of both text and music. 'We had a permanent interactive influence on each other,' he says. 'If Claude-Michel violently disliked anything I had written, however strongly I might feel about this part of the text, it was almost always discarded. He was equally responsive to what I had to say about the music.' This process took two years, resulting, finally, in a two-hour long demonstration tape produced and financed by Boublil and Schönberg, with Claude-Michel singing all the parts and accompanying himself on the piano. Jean-Marc Natel, a poet, collaborated with Boublil and Schönberg on the lyrics and has a co-writer's credit. Another essential collaborator was John Cameron, who orchestrated the score: recordings took place not in Paris, but at the CTS studio in Wembley.

John Cameron, musical supervisor and orchestrator

The record, with the famous lithograph of Cosette on the cover, was finally released in 1980, selling 260,000 copies. In September of the same year a stage version, directed by veteran French director Robert Hossein, was put on at the Palais des Sports and was seen by 500,000 people. The only interest from abroad came from the Santa Barbara Opera House wanting to put on the French *Les Misérables* with an American cast, for a few performances. It was then that Peter Farago, a young Hungarian-born director, was bowled over by the French *Les Misérables* record and decided to do something about it.

## Cameron Mackintosh

At the age of eight, Cameron Mackintosh was taken to a matinée performance of Julian Slade's musical, *Salad Days*. This childhood experience changed the course of his life. After the show, he recalls, instead of leaving with the rest of the audience, he marched down the theatre aisle, with his mother and aunt in tow, towards Julian Slade, who was still in the orchestra pit, and said he had some questions for him.

Mackintosh's purpose was entirely practical: one of the stars of *Salad Days* – a delightfully whimsical musical comedy and enormous West End hit – was a magic piano, and Mackintosh wanted to know if it was real.

*Overleaf*: 'End of the Day', Vienna

'I was confronted by this small boy in a kilt with black-rimmed spectacles and a mop of black hair,' says Slade. 'I took him on to the stage. "You'd better have a look at it," I said. He looked inside it, struck a few notes, which didn't, of course, produce a sound. I showed him my own piano hidden in the orchestra pit which I actually played during the show in the place of the dummy stage piano, and explained how everything was done. He turned to me with a huge grin on his face and said: "I *thought* it was you".'

Mackintosh recalls the moment well. 'I stood in the centre of the stage and said to myself, I wouldn't mind doing this when I grow up.'

From that time onwards, Mackintosh's life was devoted to the theatre. 'I was obsessed,' he remembers. 'I subscribed at school to theatre magazines and newspapers like "The Stage" and put on shows. I was such a salesman and became so skilled at conning local theatres and trades-people into loaning me lights and props that my nickname at Prior Park College was Darryl F. Mackintosh.'

Though Mackintosh's part Maltese, part French and part Italian mother had been the private secretary of a famous British actor, Nigel Patrick, he had no other theatrical background. His Scottish father was the manager of a timber firm and part-time amateur jazz musician. Both parents were supportive of their son's theatrical ambitions, but understandably sceptical too. Slade, who remained a close friend to Mackintosh during his schooldays, advised him to try for a place in one of the two British universities specialising in theatre – Birmingham and Bristol. Mackintosh failed to gain a place in either. Instead, he enrolled in London's Central School of Speech and Drama, but left after a year, determined to work, in any capacity, in 'real' theatre.

He did the rounds of every single theatre in London, eventually landing a temporary job (at £7 a week) as a stage-hand at the Theatre Royal, Drury Lane. The job was supposed to last only two weeks, but Mackintosh also started work there as a cleaner. *Camelot* had just opened there, and Mackintosh stayed with it for several months, making himself indispensable in all sorts of ways. Other jobs followed in other theatres: he was promoted to assistant stage manager for the national tour of Lionel Bart's *Oliver!* (which included an on-stage part in the chorus) and his real career began. 'I had wanted to be a producer since I was eight years old,' says Mackintosh, 'and I was determined to become one by the age of twenty-five. [He actually achieved this goal five years ahead of schedule.] To do that I knew I first had to gain experience in every single backstage job.'

From 1966 onwards he did just that. Working in an Emile Littler show, he started handling bookings, publicity, tours, as well as writing and editing programme notes and developing an interest in theatre poster design. It was at this time that he first met Russ Eglin, who remains one of his oldest friends. He would later design the famous *Cats*, *Phantom of the Opera* and *Les Misérables* posters and supervise all the artwork involved in other Cameron Mackintosh shows.

While working at the Palace Theatre, Mackintosh had met a young producer, Robin Alexander, and in 1967 he joined his production company. They put on five plays at the Kenton Theatre in Henley with a tiny subsidy from affluent local gentry. By 1968 he had a cramped two-room office in London's Charing Cross Road, and had begun staging low-budget repertory productions in suburban and provincial theatres. In 1969 he finally achieved his avowed ambition since the age of eight and tackled a musical. 'I had been brought up in the heyday of the American musical,' he recalls, 'and decided to put on Cole Porter's "Anything Goes" at London's Saville Theatre.'

The show was an unmitigated disaster that would dog Mackintosh's career for several years. The director and the leading lady resigned. The cast of forty was far more expensive than he had anticipated, and his £15,000 budget far too low. Costs rapidly escalated to £45,000. 'Three weeks into the show, everything bad that could possibly happen to a producer had happened to me,' Mackintosh remembers.

His basic mistake was under-capitalisation. He forgot the old theatrical adage: it's not what a show costs to put on that's important, but what it costs to take it off. After it closed, to abominable reviews and sparse audiences, Mackintosh was left with a £20,000 debt and no assets whatsoever. He began making plans to pay back the money (to an understanding bank manager) but his next venture, a stage adaptation of the famous BBC radio soap, *Mrs Dale's Diary*, was almost as unsuccessful. 'We had opened at the Winter Garden Theatre in Blackpool which has 2500 seats,' recalls Mackintosh. 'The first night our box office takings amounted to just over £10, with less than a hundred people in the audience. For the whole week, we took in £220.'

The same sympathetic bank manager now gave Mackintosh some precious advice: 'You're broke, and you owe us a fortune,' he told him, 'but if you don't pay the actors you'll never get back in the theatre. Here's another £500.'

'I knew I'd have to stop producing for a bit,' says Mackintosh. He became advertising manager for *Hair* but by 1971 he was back in business, first with a series of touring plays, mostly previous London successes, and then, in 1972, after a tour of *Salad Days*, came Julian Slade's musical, *Trelawney*, which had a reasonably successful run in London. The following year, he put on another musical, *The Card*, which ran for about six months with a strong cast headed by Jim Dale and

*Overleaf:* 'Surely something's slipped your mind', Los Angeles

Millicent Martin and choreographed by Gillian Lynne who would later work on many other Mackintosh shows, including *Cats*.

During the next few years he mounted dozens more touring productions including *Godspell*, which ran for over five years. Finally, in 1976 he had his first major international success – *Side by Side with Sondheim* which a number of theatrical entrepreneurs had avoided as a non-commercial proposition. It was *Side by Side* that caused him to be noticed: 'That was the one other producers had turned down and I'd taken a flier,' he says. 'People started saying, "maybe he'll make it after all".'

By now Mackintosh had a small office in the Phoenix Theatre, and as if to make up for past disasters, success followed success. He put together three highly successful musical-theatre productions which settled in London for long runs after initial touring try-outs: *Oklahoma*, *My Fair Lady* and *Oliver!* – ironically, the same *Oliver!* that Boublil saw in London triggering his decision to embark on *Les Misérables*. Both *My Fair Lady* (directed by Alan Jay Lerner) and *Oklahoma* were completely new productions, not in any way remakes, and all three musicals were reviewed in their own right to as much critical acclaim as the original versions. Another success was Tom Lehrer's *Tomfoolery* which opened in London and eventually off-Broadway.

While working on *Tomfoolery* in 1980, Mackintosh received a phone call from Andrew Lloyd Webber, now a major international star following the success of both *Jesus Christ Superstar* and *Evita*. He suggested they work together. Their first joint venture was what has now become the legendary *Cats*. Mackintosh had succeeded in getting Arts Council money to put on *Oklahoma* and *My Fair Lady* and believes this influenced Webber's choice. As Webber put it, 'Anyone who can get money out of the Arts Council for a musical can't be entirely stupid.'

*Cats* was regarded by most experienced members of London's theatrical 'establishment' as a maverick project designed to bankrupt whoever produced it. It was a musical without a plot, with lyrics based on the poems of one of the world's most highbrow writers, T. S. Eliot. Its director, Trevor Nunn, whom Mackintosh introduced to Andrew Lloyd Webber, had never directed a musical before. Many of Mackintosh's backers who had got substantial returns from his last two shows refused to have anything to do with this one; some thought he was crazy to tackle such an arcane subject, others stayed away for a variety of reasons, including an allergy to cats. It turned out, of course, to be an international success, still showing around the world nearly ten years after its première.

Mackintosh took *Cats* to Broadway and followed it up with the off-Broadway *Little Shop of Horrors* which he helped co-produce. Soon he had three shows running in New York simultaneously – *Cats*, *Little Shop of Horrors* and *Tomfoolery*. Thus, on the eve of embarking on *Les Misérables*, Cameron Mackintosh was an established, highly successful theatrical producer, his earlier fiascos forgotten. *Phantom of the Opera* which he would later produce with Andrew Lloyd Webber's Really Useful Group was still in the distant future.

It was in November 1982, that Peter Farago, who had been trying to develop an English-language version of *Les Misérables*, without success, took the French record round to Mackintosh and begged him to listen to it . . .

'Come on Fantine, let's have all the news', Los Angeles

'Right my girl, on your way', Norway
*Opposite*: 'I Dreamed a Dream', Patti LuPone as Fantine, London, 1985

# *From* Les Misérables *to* 'Les Mis'

'It was an instant combustible decision,' says Cameron Mackintosh. 'By the fourth track I was wildly excited and one November morning [1982] I called Alan Jay Lerner and asked to come round and see him.'

Lerner, the world-famous *My Fair Lady* lyricist, was then living in London, newly married to Liz Robertson, the Eliza Doolittle of the production he had directed, for Mackintosh. With some reason – having introduced them – Mackintosh regarded himself as something of a matchmaker.

At Lerner's Chelsea house they listened to the record. 'Lerner thought it was a marvellous piece of work but, as he put it, "it's not for me because I don't write about those sorts of people." He did say: "you must press on with this".'

Unknown to Mackintosh, someone else had been interested in an English-language version of *Les Misérables* for over a year: this was the Broadway theatre owner James Nederlander, for whom British agent, Patricia Macnaughton, acted as consultant and talent-spotter. Macnaughton had not seen the Palais des Sports show but had heard the original French record and, in 1980, flew to Paris to see Boublil. Before she left, she said to Nederlander, 'If you love and trust me, you've got to take an option on it.' Nederlander promised to pay $5000 for a one-year option. Boublil and Schönberg accepted.

This was the start of talk of an English-language adaptation, with Tim Rice, Herbert Kretzmer and Don Black mentioned as possible lyricists. But nothing more happened. By the time Cameron Mackintosh had heard the record and decided he wanted to put it on stage, the option had lapsed – without in fact ever being paid.

So, having listened to the French record, it was natural for Mackintosh to team up with Nederlander, who owned some of Broadway's most prestigious theatres. Initially, the arrangement was that Mackintosh and Nederlander would co-produce the English-language version of *Les Misérables* in London. At this stage, Peter Farago hoped he would get to direct it, though Mackintosh had made no formal promises, and had, in fact, told him, at their first meeting, that if he insisted there be a link between him and the *Les Misérables* project he wouldn't even listen to the record. So eager was Farago, however, that he had already started work on an English-language adaptation and he duly delivered a synopsis to Cameron Mackintosh at the end of 1982.

Mackintosh had other ideas though: he had been impressed by the originality of Jonathan Miller's production of the opera *Rigoletto* at the London Coliseum not long before – especially by the fresh, contemporary English lyrics, freely adapted from the Italian by James Fenton, one of Britain's leading poets and *Sunday Times* drama critic. 'It was very special,' Mackintosh recalls. 'It had the kind of appeal that attracted young people who would not usually go to the opera.' Mackintosh and Fenton got together for lunch. 'I had never met him before,' says Mackintosh. 'I was a little diffident about offering him the job since I knew of his reputation as a poet and felt he might sniff at writing a musical.' Fenton, however, accepted without hesitation.

In January 1983, a formal Nederlander-Mackintosh agreement was worked out with Paul Woerner, then Nederlander's lawyer, at a meeting in London. This set up a joint venture, with Mackintosh producing the English-language version of *Les Misérables* in Britain and Nederlander financing the Broadway production with Mackintosh as line (or executive) producer. Mackintosh's participation was also welcomed in the American financing.

Discussions now focused on the choice of director; Mackintosh had formed a definite opinion in this respect. He liked Peter Farago and had heard good things about the latter's direction of *Candide* at the Edinburgh Festival, but he saw *Les Misérables* as a spectacular show and wondered whether Farago really had sufficient experience for that. On hearing the score, Mackintosh had immediately thought of Trevor Nunn. It was, in many ways, an obvious choice. Nunn and his co-director, John Caird, had staged the memorable Royal Shakespeare Company (RSC) 8½-hour theatre adaptation of Charles Dickens' *Nicholas Nickleby*, also, like *Les Misérables*, a mammoth, classic novel with a large number of characters and complicated subplots; he had directed Mackintosh's first international musical hit, *Cats*. 'I went round for breakfast to Cameron's flat,' says Nunn, 'and he played me the record. Before he did so, we talked about the novel itself. I had to confess I'd never read it. Cameron then proceeded to tell me the story of "Les Misérables". He said it was essentially a story about a convict hunted and chased for the whole of his life by an obsessed policeman. It's a nineteenth-century version of "The Fugitive", he said. Subsequently, I discovered that Cameron had not read "Les Misérables" either, and that his was a somewhat inaccurate digest. There are more strands to the story than that. Nevertheless, I think that conversation left an impression of a very simple, theatrical, dramatic motor force, and I suspect *that* stayed with me longer than the impression of the original recording.'

Soon after that breakfast session, Mackintosh sent Nunn a

A working lunch, July 1984 (*left to right*: Trevor Nunn, James Fenton, John Caird and Cameron Mackintosh)

Trevor Nunn

*Overleaf*: 'Lovely Ladies', London

tape of the French record. 'Trevor must have been getting offers by the score,' says Mackintosh. 'I didn't hear from him for months.' It wasn't until April 1983, after numerous phone calls, that Mackintosh and Trevor Nunn talked seriously about *Les Misérables*. At first Nunn was hesitant, but a few weeks later he told Mackintosh, 'I keep listening to the tape in my car and can't get the tunes out of my head. I'll do it.' Patricia Macnaughton then had the thankless task of breaking the news to Farago that he would not, after all, be directing 'Les Mis', offering him, on Nederlander's and Mackintosh's behalf, a financial settlement based on the estimated eventual earnings of the show, which, by the end of 1989 had topped $250,000 and is still accruing. Farago accepted, though with some bitterness at first. Patricia Macnaughton kept Boublil and Schönberg informed of these negotiations. As she bluntly put it to them, if they stuck with Farago, there would probably be no London production. Aware of Nunn's past work and reputation, the two Frenchmen eagerly endorsed Mackintosh's choice.

It wasn't only the press of offers that held Nunn back at first, but the knowledge that, compelling though the original Schönberg music was, 'it would need a huge amount of work'. 'The original record,' says Nunn, 'had the slightly deceptive excitement of a very vigorous opening, the factory song, immediately followed by a song called "La Misère" which was the leitmotiv of the entire show, and this was followed, very soon afterwards, by the song that eventually became "I Dreamed a Dream". It all seemed very dramatic and invigorating, but it became repetitive and disappointing – very French in a pejorative way. After getting a translation of the original libretto, I became a little more interested, but found some difficulty in relating the language of the songs to Victor Hugo's book. It was clear that something had hooked me, and I told Cameron, "this is something I want to develop, but it should be done with a team I'm familiar with, over a long period, as an ongoing project".'

Trevor Nunn had another request: that John Caird, the Royal Shakespeare Company director with whom he had staged *Nicholas Nickleby*, be brought in as co-director. 'There were several reasons,' says Nunn. 'I had enjoyed working with Caird on "Merry Wives of Windsor" and on "Peter Pan" as well as on "Nicholas Nickleby". I knew a tremendous amount of adaptational work would have to take place. John and I not only enjoyed doing that but had developed a technique – talking things through, acting passages to each other; I also felt it would be dishonest to use methods and approaches developed during the work on "Nicholas Nickleby" and to exclude John from this process.' *Les Misérables*, Trevor Nunn realised, had to be developed 'learning all the lessons' that *Nicholas Nickleby* had taught them.

John Caird

Implicit in Trevor Nunn's commitment was the non-negotiable request that *Les Misérables* start its life as an RSC venture: 'Cameron was, of course, thinking in terms of a commercial proposition with rehearsal dates, theatres and so on. He too needed time to think about the validity of what I was saying. He had to ask himself, "Do I want to go through the business of losing an element of control?" Cameron decided to go ahead along these lines. I said, "That's a very important decision. It means that from now on – to be unveiled at the Barbican – the work is going to have a level of seriousness to meet RSC standards."'

Though the arrangements between Mackintosh and the RSC were not entirely defined in formal, legal terms, Trevor Nunn obtained the equivalent of a film director's 'final cut' approval, while the responsibility for choosing actors and musicians was to be Mackintosh's. 'We made it very clear,' says Mackintosh, 'that we wouldn't necessarily take RSC musicians unless they met with our musical director's approval. The RSC had made pacts in the past with commercial producers, but what it had never done was to actively produce inside one of their theatres with a commercial producer. I was in control, though, working hand in glove with the RSC departments, and I could, in a crisis, overrule them. The casting decisions were ours.'

At the back of Mackintosh's mind was the fear that, for all the RSC's classical theatre expertise and reputation, in-house musical theatre might be regarded by some of its members as a kind of light-hearted intermezzo, an end-of-term lark. 'We didn't want that traditional, slightly amateurish British aspect of musical theatre where brilliant classical actors let their hair down. We saw "Les Mis" as musical theatre with performers at the height of their powers combined with a classical theatre also at the height of its powers.'

At first, the invasion of the RSC by a commercial company led to some friction, and some established RSC staffers never quite adjusted to it. Trevor Nunn, however, did. A further, compelling reason for his enthusiasm in co-directing *Les Misérables* was the fact that for years, the RSC had toyed with the idea of staging an original musical, and had been looking for a suitable vehicle. There was the additional advantage of filling the large Barbican Theatre for at least two months without any direct disbursements, and the possibility of royalties if the show did well. As Artistic Director of the RSC Nunn had to get the project approved by its planning committee; its members voted unanimously in favour. Mackintosh, as well as Nunn, had good reason to welcome the inclusion of John Caird in the team for he was no newcomer and had directed a successful musical for Mackintosh – *Song and Dance* – in 1982.

All theatre deals involve the equivalent of games of musical

'You're no grander than the rest of us', Vienna
*Opposite*: 'I've seen your face before', First National Company, USA

chairs. Outstanding directors and performers are in such short supply that their availability can never be taken for granted until they have actually signed their contracts, and theatres ear-marked for specific shows often become unavailable if a successful run lasts longer than expected. But even by normal musical theatre standards, the making of *Les Misérables* was fraught with crisis. For no sooner had Trevor Nunn committed himself to direct *Les Misérables* within the R S C framework than Mackintosh started having second thoughts about his American partner, Nederlander.

The Nederlanders and the Shuberts are the twin royal families of Broadway. Mackintosh had at first welcomed Nederlander's American partnership because of his chain of theatres and the considerable capital resources at his disposal. But in the months leading up to the *Les Misérables* production, Mackintosh took a closer look at Nederlander's operations, and did not find them to his liking: while the *Les Misérables* project was still in gestation, Mackintosh produced a Broadway version of *Oliver!* at his partner's invitation and found, to his distress, that he kept clashing with 'Jimmy' Nederlander. Mackintosh is a meticulous, finicky producer, with an almost maniacal sense of detail. He was, therefore, outraged by what he regarded as corner-cutting, and by Nederlander's somewhat haphazard working methods, and especially by the speed with which he had been compelled to put on *Oliver!* in one of Nederlander's theatres. 'I was given eight weeks from start to finish,' he says. 'It simply wasn't enough.'

*Oliver!* flopped, and the Mackintosh-Nederlander relationship soured. After a series of increasingly acrimonious discussions, Nederlander agreed to pull out of the *Les Misérables* project altogether as a producer, though he offered to co-operate in finding Mackintosh a suitable Broadway theatre in which to stage it.

Thus, in the first few months following his decision to go ahead with 'Les Mis', Mackintosh had already bypassed a director as well as a co-producing partner. On the plus side, however, he was delighted with the teamwork of Nunn and Caird, on the one hand, and the original creators of 'Les Mis' – Boublil and Schönberg – on the other. The two Frenchmen had a reputation for being 'difficult', and Mackintosh had not yet actually met either of them. He flew to Paris, meeting first with Boublil, then a few weeks later, with Schönberg as well, at a fashionable Paris restaurant, 'where Claude-Michel pretended to speak no English as he sized me up'.

After several meetings in Paris and London, the French composer-librettist team was bowled over by the professionalism of Mackintosh, Nunn and Caird. 'From the word go,' says Boublil, 'we found ourselves in another world. We didn't know who Cameron Mackintosh was at first. I wasn't even aware he

Trevor Nunn and John Caird
in rehearsal

was the producer of the "Oliver!" I'd seen. He could have proposed to buy the rights of our "Les Misérables", and that's what we expected him to do – had he made us an offer, I think we would have refused to part with them. Instead, he made us a completely unexpected proposal: "I think you're the right people to do the British version," he said. "It's not just a question of adaptation. Are you prepared to start from the very beginning, all over again?" We said we were.'

By this time the *Les Misérables* production and venue plans were shaping up: it was understood that *Les Misérables* should have its première, and initial run, at the RSC's Barbican Theatre, but that the standards and rules applied should be those of commercial theatre, and that the set should be compatible with a West End transfer. Mackintosh also insisted that all RSC performers in the 'Les Mis' cast agree to stay on after the initial Barbican run, for at least twelve months.

Alain Boublil and Claude-Michel Schönberg outside the Barbican Theatre, London, 1985

The amount of work involved in getting *Les Misérables* ready for the Barbican was enormous. As Boublil and Schönberg readily admitted, their experience of musical theatre was limited – and the Palais des Sports lacked the kind of facilities that London musical theatre takes for granted. This, for them, had conditioned the text and the music from the start. 'There was no sewer scene, for instance, in the original French version', says Boublil, 'because we knew that there was no way of making such a scene credible on the platform of the Palais des Sports. It would have looked grotesque.'

Apart from one sound recording engineer, Andrew Bruce, and orchestrator, John Cameron, none of those involved in the English-language *Les Misérables* project had ever seen the French stage version though they were, of course, familiar with the French record. There were other fundamental difficulties involved in adapting the French-language *Les Misérables*. 'I found the original record very exciting,' says Caird. 'Obviously there was something there that was very theatrical, but the libretto, in French, was difficult to understand because it was so full of French colloquialisms and literary allusions. We had a literal translation done into English and it was clear that a major piece of restructuring was needed. Because Trevor Nunn and I had been involved in "Nicholas Nickleby", we saw it from the start as a very big project, and we knew that the only way we could work on it was to go back to Victor Hugo's book and start again, however much of the French version we would end up using. It was clear from the start that the French version was not performable as it stood as a mere English adaptation.'

It wasn't just the allusive language and the colloquialisms, however, that made a completely new version necessary. 'More fundamentally,' says Caird, 'there simply wasn't enough of the story on stage, the whole thing was framed in a way that was

The runaway cart, Australia

Fantine's death, Toronto
*Opposite*: 'Who am I? 24601!' Broadway

comprehensible only to an audience that was intimately aware of the story, and the traditions of English story-telling were completely absent from it.'

Before Nunn and Caird entered the picture (in the summer of 1982), Mackintosh had been working directly with James Fenton on the artistic side. Now, with the directors in place, Mackintosh started concentrating on the business aspects of the production, while Nunn, Caird, Boublil and Schönberg began working closely with Fenton. As *Sunday Times* drama critic, Fenton was well aware of Nunn's brilliance and total dedication to his craft. There was an additional link between Fenton and the Nunn–Caird team, stretching back into the distant past: both Caird and Fenton had grown up in Oxford together, where both their fathers had been Professors of Theology at Oxford University.

Fenton set about his new assignment with his characteristic loner's idiosyncrasy, taking the English translation of Victor Hugo's mammoth work on a two-month trip to Borneo with Oxford scholar-scientist Redmond O'Hanlon. Later, O'Hanlon wrote about their saga among the head-hunters in the mountains of Batu Tiban in his hilarious bestseller, *Into the Heart of Borneo*. Fenton read *Les Misérables* in early 1983 at intervals between fighting off leeches, mosquitoes and killer ants and wrestling with flooded dug-out canoes on an unrelieved diet of soggy rice and bony riverfish. To lighten his pack, he would rip off the pages of his paperback edition of *Les Misérables* after reading them and drop them in the river. Mackintosh, Nunn, Caird, Boublil and Schönberg, meanwhile, all impatiently awaited his return, for *Les Misérables* was due tentatively to open at the Barbican Theatre in the autumn of 1984.

Meanwhile, Trevor Nunn and John Caird had also read Victor Hugo's novel very carefully indeed. 'Reading the novel and listening to the original French record,' says Trevor Nunn, 'it was pretty clear they were such utterly different experiences that they shouldn't really be sharing the same title. The Paris musical could by rights be called "Scenes from 'Les Misérables'" or "A Musical Impression of 'Les Misérables'" because there the adaptation didn't begin until Valjean had changed his name and was living in Montreuil, and it ended on the barricades, with Javert's suicide and the impression left was that Valjean will somehow rescue Marius and that everything will turn out right in the end.' The French version was adapted in this way because, as Boublil points out, French audiences were so familiar with the book that they would grow impatient if they were taken through the whole story. 'The wonderful thing about Alain Boublil and Claude-Michel Schönberg,' says Nunn, 'is that they were genuine collaborators, once they were convinced they were dealing with sensible people as dedicated as themselves. They were extremely flexible, always saying, "forget about the French version".'

When Fenton finally did return to England, he said that a prologue was essential, bringing in two important elements that had not been in the French musical version: the gaol where Valjean undergoes hard labour, and the bishopric of Digne, where he repays the saintly bishop's hospitality by stealing his candlesticks. This required stylised, rapid changes of scene, which in turn determined Trevor Nunn's inspired use of what came to be one of 'Les Mis's' features – the revolving stage.

Fenton wrote most of the prologue in Stockholm, where Caird was a guest director of the Staatsteater for a Swedish adaptation of Shakespeare's *As You Like It*. Swedish theatre union rules are weighted drastically in favour of actors: rehearsals are limited to four hours a day. Fenton, therefore, worked on his own in the mornings, and later in the day he and Caird would get together and go over what he had written. The ideas and shape of the first twenty minutes of 'Les Mis', telling the story of Jean Valjean's early life, are, as Mackintosh and all involved in the English-language production concur, very much inspired by James Fenton, as was the idea for the *Café Song* in the second act, with its lament for Marius's dead comrades (this eventually became *Empty Chairs at Empty Tables*). 'His contribution to these essential changes was vital,' says Mackintosh.

As Nunn and Caird started mulling over Victor Hugo's narrative – and comparing it to the Boublil–Schönberg French musical version – they too had important suggestions for change: none of the characters, with the possible exception of Fantine, they felt, had any real dramatic life: they were all stereotypes, written as characters in a melodrama. As Caird put it, 'You can't ask an actor to play a part if it isn't there, and you can't ask an audience to watch the development of a character if there's never a moment when the essence of that character is communicated to the spectators.' The French musical version, says Caird, 'was basically a series of tableaux in the French tradition interpolated by large-scale pieces of symphonic music in order to prepare for set changes, so there were some great long interludes which none of us in London felt were useable. Boublil and Schönberg came around to this, accepting our points by stages, but they were not, at first perhaps, aware of how major the changes we sought to make were. They did, however, accept them unreservedly.'

With their story-telling experience as co-directors of the famous *Nicholas Nickleby* production, Trevor Nunn and John Caird wanted the *story* of *Les Misérables* to emerge more clearly and much more dramatically. 'Having read the book,' Caird says, 'I was reassured that we weren't doing something crazy. Victor Hugo's novel is nowhere near as complex as "Nicholas

*Overleaf*: 'Master of the House', London

Nickleby" or most of Dickens' major novels. It is much simpler to tell. For all its length, it is basically a story of intimate human relations, paralleled by the history of France. Sometimes the two sit well together, sometimes they merely run in parallel. There's no attempt, on Hugo's part, to tell the story of the history of France through a wealth of character detail as Dickens would have done. Though it's called "Les Misérables", there are very few actual "miserables" in the story itself – it's mostly to do with student-class intellectuals, criminals, profiteers. There are all sorts of different people, but the abject poor are not characterised. If you try and reduce the plot of a Dickens novel to a few lines, you find it's really irreducible, for you've got to introduce the subplots in order to tell the whole story. Victor Hugo's "Les Misérables" can be summarised in two or three sentences very easily.'

In a Dickens story, Caird points out, again basing his comments on his *Nicholas Nickleby* experience, 'there are usually fifty to sixty irreducibly important characters'. In Hugo's *Les Misérables* there are far less; in his original story, Hugo used the novelist's time-honoured device of introducing a character, and then, in a flashback, telling his readers all about that character's antecedents, sometimes going back several generations. Thus, Marius Pontmercy is seen, at first, through his father, the Bonapartist general (who was robbed of his watch by Thénardier as he lay dying on the field of Waterloo), and we end up knowing a great deal about the Pontmercy family, for there are several chapters devoted to Marius's grandfather. Fantine first appears, in the book, as one of the young working girls taken up by a group of students in Paris, who then cruelly abandon them once they've completed their studies. None of these minor characters were essential to the telling of the story on stage.

There was, however, a strong theme in Hugo's novel that Trevor Nunn and John Caird both felt lacking in the original French musical version and which they thought had to be stressed: the religious statement. 'Javert,' says Nunn, 'is someone who believes in a vengeful, Old Testament God who will bring down plague and pestilence on all those who disobey the law; Valjean, in the light of his own experiences, has come to believe in redemption and that justice can exist in our world; Thénardier not only believes that God is dead but that he died a long time ago and that we are all fair game for him.'

All this, the two directors believed, needed to be stated, both musically and theatrically and their feeling was endorsed, once rehearsals had started, by the performers themselves, who wanted their parts strengthened in the second act. Three songs sung by the major characters do, in fact, embody Hugo's essential themes: in 'Bring Him Home', Valjean introduces the notion of New Testament mercy; in 'Stars', Javert explains why, in his high-principled but warped mind, religion is indissolubly linked with order, and in 'Dog Eat Dog', Thénardier states his predatory view of the world. 'All this explains why we ended up with a three-hour version,' says Caird. 'The difference between the two is much greater than simply adding another hour's worth of material.'

As time went on, Mackintosh, Nunn, Caird, Boublil and Schönberg all started getting anxious: Fenton was moving ahead with his version of the libretto with agonising slowness. By January 1984, Mackintosh had hoped to start casting for an October 1984 opening, but it soon became clear that this would have to be postponed for a year: there was no script.

'We cruised through 1984,' Mackintosh recalls. 'As a drama critic, James came to terms with deadlines, but he is by nature a loner and a perfectionist. He felt there was plenty of time, and that endless revisions were all part of the creative process. He simply had to work at his own pace. Alain and Claude-Michel brought him over to Paris, and we all tried to hurry him along. But James is not by nature a collaborator, and his reaction to our chivvying was to say, "Don't worry, in order to produce the best possible script no short-cuts are possible".'

There were other problems. Though all involved felt the prologue was superb, Mackintosh, and, even more so, Trevor Nunn, had reservations about some of Fenton's ever-distinguished, highly polished writing. Their basic criticism was that it was *too* poetic, too intellectual, and in parts just not singable. 'James became increasingly locked in his own world,' says Mackintosh. 'He took kindly to suggestions, but felt quite strongly about some things. There was much interesting writing, but it would have sung in a somewhat archaic, over-intellectualised language. We wanted something contempor-ary. James's sense of language was highly individual and esoteric, allusive, for me at least somewhat over-literary. I started getting concerned. He had been at work for over a year and a half and was only half-way through the script when we began having these mounting reservations. Eventually we all realised that – at the pace it was evolving – we wouldn't be able to start casting by April 1985, and that the autumn opening, already delayed by a year, might be in jeopardy for 1985. Trevor Nunn agreed with me. Something had to be done.'

'What was emerging from James Fenton in Oxford,' says Nunn, 'was hybrid and at times unsingable. He appeared to be falling between two stools. He was full of ideas that would have taken off if he had been starting from scratch – with the music to come later on – but he seemed to be confined by the existing musical format. He wanted more space, and more time to work his ideas out. I sensed he could have written a whole volume of poems about "Les Misérables" and his reaction to it.' Reluc-tantly, Mackintosh and Nunn decided to change writers in

Herbert Kretzmer

'Master of the House', Japan

'. . . watering the wine', Oslo

Claude-Michel Schönberg

midstream. Herbert Kretzmer, veteran songwriter, lyricist, former drama critic for the *Daily Express* and *Daily Mail* television critic, now came aboard.

Though Kretzmer had, in fact, been approached two years earlier by Patricia Macnaughton, there had been no follow-up. In mid-1984 he had, quite coincidentally, approached Mackintosh to find out whether he would be interested in reviving Kretzmer's own past work, *Our Man Crichton* (based on J. M. Barrie's play, *The Admirable Crichton*). Kretzmer had been writing lyrics and songs ever since his South African student days, and had worked closely with the French singer Charles Aznavour, adapting the latter's songs from French to English with considerable success. Now, in January 1985, Mackintosh remembered Kretzmer's work, especially his faculty of adapting French lyrics into English, and asked him whether he was prepared to rewrite *Les Misérables* – fast.

It had been Mackintosh's and Nunn's original intention to ask Kretzmer and Fenton to work together, but – aware that Fenton was very much a loner – Kretzmer believed it would be simpler to work on his own. 'We wanted to keep what James Fenton had to offer us and prevent someone from hitting the panic button,' says Nunn. 'John Caird and I wanted Kretzmer to join the team and we tried to define various ways in which this could happen.' But it was soon clear that with Fenton's methods this would not be possible. 'Mackintosh summoned me to his office', says Fenton, 'and fired me. Contractually, he was within his rights, but it was quite a painful experience just the same.'

'I started on March 1 and from that moment onwards rarely stepped out of my Basil Street flat except to attend rehearsals,' says Kretzmer. 'Because I lived near the Harrods Food Hall, and I knew Claude-Michel's fondness for smoked salmon, we got through mountains of the stuff before it was all over. I have never worked so hard in my life.'

There was an enormous amount of writing to be done: Fenton had not gone much beyond the first act, though he had mapped out some of the barricades lyrics. 'What I was engaged in can't in any way be called translation,' says Kretzmer. 'A third of the work to be done consisted of a *form* of translation, a third was free adaptation, with completely new words to existing music, and a third of it involved writing completely new songs.'

Neither 'Stars' (Javert's soliloquy), nor 'Carousel' (the women's reflection of the students' sacrifice at the barricades) nor the rollicking ballroom scene and song at the end of the second act existed in the original version. In the French, the music for the prostitutes' song, 'Lovely Ladies', had had no erotic connotations whatsoever (it had been called 'La Nuit' – The Night). The Cosette song, 'Castle On a Cloud', had completely different lyrics and so had 'On My Own', Éponine's song, originally (in the French version) sung by Fantine.

The well-known lyricist Don Black has described writing lyrics as, 'the most painful process there is – rather like doing your own root canal work'. 'It's uphill work all the way,' agrees Kretzmer, 'and quite different from writing poetry. It's a separate discipline, which is why most song lyrics don't look good in print. The lyric writer's first obligation is to be singable. He is as much concerned with sound as he is with sense. There are certain sounds that cannot, or should not, be sung. A line with too many "ss"s in it, for instance, should at all costs be avoided, because it's bound to emerge on stage as an incomprehensible series of sibilants, especially when sung by a chorus of voices. Again, it is unfair and impractical to ask a singer to sing a word like "me" on a high, sustained note, because unlike the other vowels, the "eee" vowel tends to close the singer's throat. The golden rule is: if it comes easily out of the singer's mouth, it will go easily into the audience's ear. Poets have greater freedom, since they work alone and don't have a rigid shape imposed on them by collaborators. You can't negotiate with form. A lyric writer follows the music or he's dead. There are certain words, for example, like "marriage" or "courage" or "tickle" where the second syllable cannot be held or extended. Writing for the musical theatre also means that your text must be instantly understood. A reader can mull over a line of poetry. Indeed, it is desirable that a poem be absorbed in silence, and at the reader's own pace. Poems don't have to be immediately accessible. But music, in a song, is relentless. You can't ask an audience to pause and reflect on a line of lyrics. You get on with it. Songs don't wait around for you while you solve their little secrets.'

Herbert Kretzmer

In the case of the lyric-writing in 'Les Mis' there were technical as well as deadline problems: 'Music may well be an international language,' says Kretzmer, 'but fashioned to accommodate the cadences of a particular tongue, it comes to possess its own codes which are not easily broken. The French language is full of emphatic consonants, staccato tricks of rhythm and fading syllables at the end of sentences which have no ready equivalents in the English language. Schönberg's score was decidedly Gallic.'

When rehearsals for 'Les Mis' finally began, in July 1985, Kretzmer was still hard at work on the lyrics, working round the clock with Claude-Michel Schönberg. Auditions were held on the basis of the performers' own material – Mackintosh was unwilling to let them sing any of the Act One lyrics which, he knew, would probably be changed as a result of Kretzmer's work. What did exist was a detailed synopsis, originally worked out by Trevor Nunn, which Boublil and the others referred to as 'the Bible'. This was practically a scene-by-scene breakdown

The young Cosette, Toronto
*Opposite*: 'I am here to help Cosette', London, 1985

of the musical's proposed dramatic structure, though, of course, many of the lyrics, especially in the second act, had still to be written.

'The second act, in a musical, is always a potential source of crisis,' says Caird. 'Having mastered their Act One parts, the actors inevitably want to feel they're given something equally important to do in the second half. Sometimes such complaints don't stem solely from actors' egos but are rooted in fact.' Soliloquies, such as 'Bring Him Home' and 'Empty Chairs', had already been deemed necessary as well as Javert's 'Stars' in the first act. It was Alun Armstrong, playing Thénardier, who was instrumental in fleshing out his own part with 'Dog Eat Dog'. The women's 'Carousel' song, after the barricades, was only written once rehearsals had started, out of sheer practical considerations: 'The women in the cast – Fantine, Cosette and Éponine apart,' says Mackintosh, 'didn't have very much to do in the second act.' Valjean's 'Bring Him Home', perhaps the most moving song of all, was devised as a much-needed lyrical moment after the excitement of the barricades' spectacular scenery change and was completed by Schönberg and Kretzmer only three weeks before the première. It was, according to Kretzmer, one of the most difficult pieces of music to set words to. Originally, the idea had been to hint at Valjean's despair at Cosette's abandoning him for a younger man. 'We wanted to evoke the natural, latent sexuality in Valjean that must have been there, however sublimated,' says Kretzmer. When Schönberg brought him the music, intensely lyrical but stark – basically the whole song revolves around the first three notes – it was clear to all that there would be no way of conveying this to that kind of music. 'Occasionally,' says Kretzmer, 'the work imposes its own rules. We couldn't do what we set out to do, but in fact came up with something better. Sometimes the music tells you what to write. In the case of "Bring Him Home", once I had realised that the song sounded like a prayer, it suddenly became clear to me that this, one of Claude-Michel's best melodies, could expose the best in Valjean and sum up his long itinerary from selfishness to altruism. Once we started conceiving the melody as a form of prayer for the life and happiness of someone else, it more or less wrote itself.' As Nunn recalls, Kretzmer finally wrote the entire text of 'Bring Him Home' overnight, 'and we immediately knew he had scored a bull's-eye.'

Another extraordinarily effective transformation came with a song sung by Fantine in the French version which, in the later stages of the Kretzmer–Schönberg partnership, became Éponine's 'On My Own' (originally 'La Misère'). 'Of all the songs in the show, this was the one that gave us the most trouble,' says Kretzmer. 'The melody is one of the seminal pieces of music in the entire show, it recurs in Fantine's death-

Barbican production meeting

bed scene, and again when Fantine appears at the very end, as a ghost, it resonates and reverberates throughout the entire evening. We discussed the text of this song for weeks, in restaurants, during rehearsal breaks. In the end everyone – Caird, Nunn, Alain – chipped in with something. To this day, I'm not certain we got it exactly right.'

Another concern, as Schönberg and Kretzmer beavered away in Basil Street, was a purely practical one: Mackintosh was adamant that *Les Misérables* could not be more than three hours long: with the future of the show far from secure and advance bookings still very slow, the cost of overtime incurred after three hours could be crippling at a time when *Les Misérables* was still struggling to find an audience. 'Life got difficult,' Kretzmer recalls. 'Trevor Nunn's patience and healing calm were never more evident. He refused to accept the conventional notion of "too long". Five minutes could be too long in a certain context, he said, five hours not long enough in others. There was a lot of heavy hustling.'

'Things did get somewhat strained,' Trevor Nunn remembers. 'Cameron wanted major cuts, which would have reduced its length to two and a half hours. I resisted, refusing to discuss things in these terms. The time did come when, as had been envisaged but, hopefully, thought unlikely to happen, when I said: the show is going to open at the Barbican under the RSC banner, and therefore it has to be a show that has my approval. If it moves to another theatre later that will be your problem. "Stars" and the "Café Song" were saved. "Stars" for me was a fundamental element of the whole show: without it Javert is a cypher, a shadowy figure, and without it there is no tragic dimension to his suicide. The song makes the audience aware of a man broken on the wheel of the intractability of his beliefs.' As Mackintosh recalls, it wasn't the song itself but its particular place in the first act that bothered him, on the grounds that it held up the narrative action. 'It took a long time for Trevor Nunn to agree but he finally concurred that it's proper place was further on in the first act,' he says. Some of the other proposed cuts – like the removal of the 'Master of the House' scene-setting preamble – were tried out in previews and then restored as the scenes would not work without them.

'Master of the House' rehearsal

The first preview was almost four hours long, but by the time of the Barbican première some thirty minutes had been removed; another five minutes were taken out between the end of the Barbican run and the Palace Theatre opening: Valjean's meeting with Cosette in the woods, the spectacular chase sequence involving Javert and Valjean, and some of Gavroche's 'Little People' song. Another five minutes were lost for the Washington opening at the Kennedy Center, and all these cuts and technical improvements were embodied in the Broadway production which has become the standard reference for all subsequent

*Overleaf*: Third National Company, USA

productions around the world. In the event, Kretzmer notes, American audiences adjusted to a three-hour show.

Given that what 'Les Mis' audiences everywhere have seen is the version completed by Herbert Kretzmer in close co-operation with Nunn, Caird, Boublil and Schönberg, it's almost impossible to imagine what a Fenton 'Les Mis' would have been like. Somewhat naturally, Fenton believes that his own version, had he been allowed to complete it, would have been superior. 'My personal impression,' he says, 'is that while both Nunn and Mackintosh argued that to work, "Les Mis" had to appeal to a vast, popular audience, they were in fact targeting the whole thing towards Broadway.' (Mackintosh denies this.) Fenton, now working for the *Independent* in South-East Asia, has not written any more for the musical theatre.

In retrospect, John Caird has had second thoughts about a few of the jettisoned Fenton lyrics. 'To say that the Fenton version would have been better than the one we ended up with is misleading,' he says. 'It wasn't just that Fenton's lyrics were not as "singable" as Kretzmer's; there weren't enough of them to make up a complete, rounded piece of musical theatre. Fenton is a poet, not a librettist. He's also a very private man, an artist who likes to take an idea away and have a long think about it and then write what he feels is the definitive version. I don't think James could have worked with the speed and felicity needed when the pressure was on. We were waiting for weeks for things that would take a professional lyricist only a few hours to achieve. Fenton would say: if you want the best, you don't do it in a few hours. But musicals are written collaboratively, often in chaos, with a lot of people suggesting things, and you have to be very fast on your feet.'

All that aside, as both Mackintosh and Caird point out, their debt to Fenton is considerable. 'He wrote what concerned him,' says Caird. 'The barricades scenes have the kind of life and vitality they do because of Fenton's experience as a foreign correspondent, drawing on the kind of violence he had seen, especially the student uprising in South Korea, where loud-hailers were also used.'

Fenton's work as a roving reporter in South-East Asia gave him a unique understanding of the have-nots – the Gavroches – of nineteenth-century Paris; he felt they weren't so very different from the have-nots of Vietnam, the Philippines, Cambodia.

Caird particularly regrets losing Fenton's immensely powerful and pertinent Gavroche lyric called, simply, 'You':

You thought you would notice we had nothing to eat.
You thought we wouldn't mind we had to sleep on the streets.
You thought you wouldn't bother if we drank from a ditch.
You thought we wouldn't wonder what had made you so rich.

You made up all the rules.
You must have thought us fools . . .
You kicked us in the gutter and you laughed in our face.
You dragged us through the courtroom and you taught us our
    place.
You preached at us on Sunday looking solemn and sleek.

You cheated us on Monday and the rest of the week.
We saw the coaches passing on the way to the ball.
I wonder if you noticed we had nothing at all.
We smelt you coming out again with brandy for breath.
I wonder if you noticed we were starving to death.

Be careful as you go.
You don't know what we know.
You drove us to despair.
You thought we didn't care.

Trevor Nunn, directing

This song, with its blend of nineteenth-century revolutionary fervour and modern radicalism, was considered too tough, too ideological for a mass-market 'Les Mis'. A pity, feels Caird. The same fate befell another of Fenton's lyrics (later replaced by the much sweeter, more sentimental Gavroche 'Little People' song – which in turn was shortened after the Barbican previews):

Ten little bullets in my hand,
ten little snipers neat and clean –
one for the king of this great land,
two for the aristocracee,
three for the bishops and the clergymen,
four for the prefects of police –

give me a chance, I'll take the lot of them –
ten little chances to be free.
Close your eyes, I'll say when, count to ten.

Such were the artistic preoccupations, the crises and inner struggles taking place behind the scenes as *Les Misérables* gradually took on its definitive form. At the same time, Mackintosh, Trevor Nunn and John Caird were assembling a cast and embarking on the equally complicated exercise of turning a musical score with words into a compellingly visual spectacle.

*Overleaf*: 'Was there a witness to this?'
Toronto

# From April '85 to Opening Night

Outsiders, brought up on classic Hollywood movies about show business, believe casting to be part of the glamorous, mythic side of theatre life. To those directly involved, however, it is an anxious, sometimes painful, and nearly always frustrating process. Casting had begun while *Les Misérables* was still being written – and in the middle of a major, though unpublicised, crisis and since both Boublil and Schönberg were contractually required to approve all decisions, the auditioning hopefuls faced a formidable array of personalities: Cameron Mackintosh, Trevor Nunn, John Caird, Alain Boublil, Claude-Michel Schönberg, musical director Martin Koch and musical supervisor (and orchestrator) John Cameron, among others. The proceedings went on for months: candidates arrived at their appointed times, sang a song of their choice, answered questions, and, if they looked promising, were put on a 'short list' for an interview. The second time, they were given some of the *Les Misérables* lyrics, but these were by no means definitive, since they were mostly Fenton's and were in the throes of being rewritten by Kretzmer, now hard at work.

Alun Armstrong and Sue Jane Tanner – the Thénardiers

One of Trevor Nunn's demands, readily conceded by Mackintosh, was that as many of the cast as possible be chosen from the ranks of the Royal Shakespeare Company. Almost immediately three RSC members landed major parts: Roger Allam as Javert, Alun Armstrong as Thénardier, and Sue Jane Tanner as Madame Thénardier. Many more could have had parts, for several members showed remarkable singing skills. But, as Caird says, 'Musical theatre attracts a special kind of person. RSC members are all highly skilled, experienced classical actors, and not many of them wanted to be anonymous members of a musical ensemble with no lines of their own, and at this stage some of the parts didn't even have character names. Those who did want to be part of "Les Mis" wanted the eight or nine principal roles, and this meant they had to be able to sing divinely.'

Several internationally known stars came to London at their own expense to audition, among them Topol, the Israeli star of *Fiddler on the Roof*, and the veteran actor Max Von Sydow. Both were keen to play Jean Valjean, but despite their outstanding acting abilities, neither was quite right for the part vocally. As casting went into its second, then third, month, there was still no outstanding candidate to play Jean Valjean. Nor was there a

Fantine. Rehearsals looked like starting without either of them, which didn't seem to faze Trevor Nunn, used to the hazards of casting; it did, however, cause Mackintosh some sleepless nights.

One of the basic rules of casting is that it's fatal to make up one's mind hastily, on the spur of the moment, or on the basis of a vague hunch; endless patience, a gambler's luck, and a fatalistic streak are required. Shortly before rehearsals started, Trevor Nunn asked Tim Rice for advice. As Rice remembers it, Nunn gave him a thumbnail description of the character of Jean Valjean as follows: 'What's needed,' he said, 'is someone who looks like a convict, is very strong, can carry a guy weighing thirteen stone on his back around the stage and still sing beautifully.' Rice immediately said, 'That's Colm Wilkinson.'

At this time Wilkinson was best known as a kind of Irish troubadour, who had been singing all over Ireland and the United States since the age of sixteen. He had been Pontius Pilate on the *Jesus Christ Superstar* record and Ché on the first *Evita* album but was not himself a star. Trevor Nunn knew of him by reputation, had heard the *Jesus Christ Superstar* record but had never met him.

'The minute you started to sing at the audition,' Trevor Nunn told Wilkinson later, 'we all knew we'd found Jean Valjean.' He sang the 'Anthem' song from *Chess*, then Schönberg took him through some of the 'Les Mis' songs in Act One. Wilkinson's natural, golden tenor voice excited all those present, though Schönberg was aware that there would be considerable musical rewriting to be done: originally Valjean had been cast as a deep baritone. Martin Koch, the musical director, and John Cameron, the orchestrator, rewrote large chunks of the music, putting it in a higher key.

So rehearsals began with Wilkinson in the principal role (he was, in fact, the last person to be cast before they started) but still without Fantine. Then Mackintosh learnt that American actress, Patti LuPone, was due to star in *The Cradle Will Rock* in London's West End and he asked Trevor Nunn whether he was interested. Patti LuPone was a 'name', the Broadway star of *Evita* and Nunn *was* enthusiastic. Mackintosh played LuPone the original French record of *Les Misérables* in New York, just before she left. 'I knew it would be a hit from listening to the first strains of the music, the sheer emotionalism of it,' she said. 'Besides, the lure of working with Trevor Nunn at the RSC was irresistible.' She auditioned, but in her case it was a mere formality. 'I knew I could do Fantine with my eyes closed,' she said. 'I'm really great in these weepy parts. The day after the opening night of "The Cradle Will Rock", I showed up for daytime rehearsals for "Les Mis", two weeks after they had already begun.'

'We started rehearsals with an extremely intelligent group of

Colm Wilkinson and Zoë Hart – Valjean and the young Cosette

Colm Wilkinson, Rebecca Caine and cast for 'One Day More'

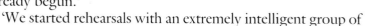

'A Heart Full of Love', Norway

*Above*: The ABC Café, Australia
*Below*: 'When tomorrow comes', Norway

Colm Wilkinson and Rebecca Caine – Valjean and Cosette

people,' Trevor Nunn recalls. 'Nobody was cast in that show simply because they had a solid background in musical theatre, but because they were immensely chameleon-like as actors and committed and aware as people. On the first day, I did a history of all French revolutions, and told them about Victor Hugo's book. The rehearsal period was very exhilarating precisely because it was so unusually serious. There was a lot of improvisational work, and a lot of it came from the novel. We extracted something like twenty paragraphs from the book which were descriptions of minor characters and we built up a series of individual improvisations, with people switching from one character to another, partly to get people to understand the nimbleness that would be required of them as actors, to populate the scenes. It was also a way of taking the cast through the experience of finding out what kind of writer Victor Hugo had been, why he was different from Dickens, what his concerns were. Our street urchin improvisations lasted a whole day. Probably the whole of the first three weeks were dominated by improvisational work, and then a certain amount of music learning. Cameron was extremely enlightened to give us a rehearsal room which had a revolve [revolving stage] in it, because none of those things could have been worked out without it.'

All successful musical theatre is dependent on teamwork. With rehearsals now under way, three members of the creative team now came into their own, and helped make 'Les Mis' what it finally became.

The key figure was, of course, John Napier, the stage designer. He had worked with Trevor Nunn before, and their combined experience on *Nicholas Nickleby* was crucial to *Les Misérables*. 'Napier and I share a vocabulary and a way of working I treasure very deeply,' says Nunn. 'It's like a marriage, we have our disagreements and our rows, but we also have moments when we are the same person. I asked John, "how do you design something that is a constant chase, that has to have, throughout, a sense of perpetual motion?" The major ingredient had to be the revolve, used in a cinematic way. We also used the revolve to say, well, you've seen the scene from this angle, how does it look from this other vantage-point? But its chief value was that here was something that the cast could walk against, that could keep the elements of the chase in dramatic motion.'

Some of Napier's inspired decisions were accidental. A very successful, intensely busy craftsman with several irons constantly in the fire, he had had no time to read Hugo's book. 'If I had, I'd still be at it,' he says. 'But by one of the flukes of life, we decided to have a weekend in Paris – Trevor, John Caird and I plus wives and girlfriends, simply to soak up the atmosphere. We visited the Victor Hugo Museum, but also wandered the

John Napier, designer

streets where the barricades, the revolutions had taken place. We soaked up the atmosphere of the old Paris, the rue Saint-Antoine, the Bastille district. Like a shot out of the blue – that second morning in Paris, we were talking, endlessly, about major problems: how do you achieve the barricades on stage? – an idea suddenly came to me. What you see on stage is basically that idea.'

The mobile barricade, with its two segments gliding spectacularly into place, gradually took shape first as a tiny model, finally becoming a reality on the huge Barbican stage. At first Napier had wanted four separate elements, but Cameron Mackintosh vetoed this on the grounds that the highly complex machinery needed to operate them could well go wrong, and that with four segments, the chances of this happening were multiplied.

In his central London studio, Napier fiddled endlessly with barricade shapes. The realisation of a concept, he says, 'is always the hard part. It was a long, complicated process, like playing with a jigsaw puzzle. We worked out where the constructed pieces should go – and where they would fit into the main frame. I was keen to use all the power on board to avoid trailing cables. The engine operating the two moving sections that join together to form the barricades had to be absolutely silent.'

The wedding ball

The engineering brain behind the actual machinery is that of Mike Barnett, a specialist completely unknown outside the theatre world but idolised by insiders. Barnett designed the machinery in his Norfolk workshop, commissioning other firms to build the hardware to his specifications. 'Designing a set for "Les Misérables",' says Napier, 'is like an architect working out the needs of a building. I did the crazy headwork, and then went to down-to-earth craftsmen who knew their figures. Barnett's immense advantage is that he never turns anything down on the grounds that it can't be done. The greater the challenge, the happier he is. In the case of the moving barricades, his very first reaction was: that's great!'

There is no gimmickry on the set of 'Les Mis', Napier maintains. 'The moving segments of the barricades served a definite purpose. What I designed was basically an all-purpose set for an epic classic, not so very different from the one I had designed for "Nicholas Nickleby".'

All Napier's stage designs are first built as miniature three-dimensional models, with actors represented by clay figures a few inches high. A former sculptor, Napier prefers modelling his sets and stage figures to drawing them. 'It's easier,' he says, 'to work out the detailed problems, and iron out the flaws. One has to ask oneself constantly: if we do this, how does it all fit in, and what is the whole going to look like?' 'Les Mis' was unusual, he adds, in that the flow of ideas, from the start, 'appeared to be all in the right direction, and nothing much had

Javert's arrest

*Overleaf*: 'Do You Hear the People Sing?' Third National Company, USA

to be discarded'. Because of the nature of his work, it wasn't until its first night that Napier actually saw – and heard – *Les Misérables* in its entirety.

The designer always influences the overall visual picture on stage, for his sets determine the predominant colours that will be seen. In the case of *Les Misérables* Napier says, 'there was one dominant colour – and that colour was grey.' The costumes were dictated by the sets, and had to blend with them, but they also had to define the actors, making them memorable in the eyes of the audience. Enter Andreane Neofitou, the costume designer trained, like Napier, at the Hornsey College of Art, and formerly married to him.

Andreane Neofitou's sketches for costume designs

Theatre costume design follows some basic rules: clothes on stage have to enable actors to move freely; they cannot differentiate too much from the period in question; and they have to fit the overall colour patterns of the sets. Napier's nineteenth-century Paris, with its emphasis on grey cobblestones, grey-granite Haussmann buildings and the sombre tones of Montreuil-sur-Mer, required clothes that would stand out without clashing stridently with the overall colour motif. Like most British-based costume designers about to start work on a period piece, Neofitou headed for the Victoria and Albert Museum library, one of the world's most comprehensive guides to clothing through the ages.

As far back as 1789, when the French Revolution began, France was already the European centre of fashion, and through the large-circulation newspapers and magazines, stored at the Victoria and Albert, 'we have a detailed knowledge of what fashionable men and women of the time wore, where hemlines stood, and what accessories they bought,' says Neofitou. Photography had not yet been invented, and would only come into its own in the 1860s, shortly before Victor Hugo's death, but the etched plates in ladies' magazines are highly reliable. There is further evidence of clothing styles and fashions in the great art of the period. Peasant and working-class clothing was a little more difficult to reconstruct, but as Neofitou points out, 'peasant costume doesn't change all that much in the ninteenth century.'

Because of her experience as a former fashion designer, she says, 'I feel I'm not a costumier, I make characters. The worst thing for me is for a costume to stick out; I want to be able to lose it and bring it out when I want to, and I want the actors to feel they're not wearing costumes but everyday clothes. Because of this I work with the actor, we develop the character through what he's doing on stage. A lot of work is immersion into a given period. If you store enough information in your head, then, hopefully, when you characterise someone, you know how they should look.'

What made 'Les Mis' special, was, she says, 'that here was a piece of musical theatre with lots of little characters, some of whom don't even say a line, they come on stage briefly and then disappear. But unless they are clearly defined in the spectator's mind they won't be memorable. Most of these company roles don't introduce themselves – as farmers, whores, convicts. The spectator has to be able to identify them from what they wear: the clothes are a short cut to the characters they express.'

The danger, of course, was that the overall colour-scheme would make for drab uniformity. Neofitou overcame this potential problem in several ways: the farmers' colours were earthy, but orange-tinged ('I wanted them to look hot, because they're in the heat, I wanted to reflect something of the ochre colour of French earth'); for the factory scene she selected a range of blue-grey shades ('a slightly soulless industrial colour'); and for the 'Lovely Ladies' scene Neofitou let her imagination run riot: 'Trevor at first wanted reality, he had visions of the whores in normal dresses of the period, but tattered and torn; I had stylised them in the erotic corsets of the time so the spectators had visions of whores, not necessarily as they looked in the 1820s but as they imagined them. Trevor said, "They look like saloon girls in a Western." I begged him to trust me. "The audience will have seen the misery of the factory, we need a break here," I said – and he finally agreed.' (Nunn describes the 'Lovely Ladies' number as 'a hideous piece of vulgarity that makes you understand what's happening to Fantine, how nothing ladylike is able to be retained.') 'The music, too,' says Neofitou, 'plays an important part in defining the colours you will use. When it's "up" you've got to help lift it visually as well.'

A further trick was to dye the clothes so that they were all of a type, but with a colour spectrum providing for minute variations, from one actor to the other. Stage clothing has to be 'distressed' to look worn, but this can only be done with natural-fibre cloth. Anything else will always look too new. This provides its own set of problems, however, because, in a long run such as that of *Les Misérables*, cloth of a given type usually runs out, and can't be duplicated exactly. In countries like the USA where natural fibres are in short supply, simply finding the right textiles in large enough quantities was to be an additional challenge.

One final problem, for Neofitou, concerned the numbers of clothes required. No two costumes could be identical, but the cast at the end of rehearsals comprised far more people than the original number budgeted for. This was because, as rehearsals proceeded, Trevor Nunn realised certain choruses had to be fleshed out with extra voices to give them greater intensity, so more players were hired, with each company member playing several parts. In 'Les Mis' there are twenty-seven adult members of the cast with some 450 separate pieces of clothing all told. Some of the actors were later heard to say they weren't in a play

*Overleaf*: 'Here a little dip, there a little touch', Third National Company, USA

Andreane Neofitou, costume designer

David Hersey, lighting designer

so much as in a quick-change fashion show! Andreane Neofitou's entire clothes budget was a modest £40,000 – 'and some of that', she says, 'was stolen for the stage design.'

The third, vital member of the creative team was American-born David Hersey, the lighting director. Theatre lighting is, perhaps, the least understood of all the theatre arts. As Hersey himself puts it, 'you can't talk about it in tangible, concrete terms,' and the jargon of lighting directors tends to be unintelligible to the layman. It's also a craft that is constantly evolving, as top men like Hersey tend to innovate all the time, making and marketing their new equipment as they go along.

Hersey and Napier worked closely together. 'Very little was planned in advance,' says Hersey. 'We simply started bringing different elements together. The Javert suicide was a problem. What we came up with was basically Napier's idea. We could have had Javert jump. Napier got the idea, very late in rehearsals, that the bridge should go up rather than Javert go down, and once that decision had been made the lighting of that particular scene became absolutely clear to me.' Hersey lit the revolve to give a whirlpool ripple impression. 'The effect grew in New York, and now we've put a centre to it, the ripple effect is increased.' Like all good things in the theatre, he says, 'this one was basically very simple.' Another spectacular success was achieved in the sewer scene with a trick combining lighting and perspective to give the impression of a vast underground tunnel.

For Hersey, prize-winning lighting director of innumerable hits including *Cats* and *Evita*, 'there is always a structure: the trick is discovering what the rules are for that particular production. Nothing necessarily carries over into other shows – though my work on "Nicholas Nickleby" was relevant, and helped.'

Like Napier, Hersey concentrated to such an extent on the visual work at hand that he never saw the entire performance from beginning to end until the opening night.

As rehearsals shifted from a hall to the giant stage of the Barbican itself, the sense of excitement among the cast was growing. 'The atmosphere was very special,' Patti LuPone recalls, 'different from any other musical I have been in.' The first time Colm Wilkinson ran through 'Bring Him Home', there was a hush throughout the theatre, eventually broken by Trevor Nunn. 'I told you the play was all about God, that it would be a deeply religious experience,' he told the assembled cast. 'Yes,' said one of the actors, 'but you didn't tell us you'd engaged Him to sing it.'

In the final three weeks prior to opening night, one of the actors recalls, everyone was living, eating and sleeping 'Les Mis'. Some musical changes were made within hours of the première. On opening night, a glittering affair with Britain's critics and theatre establishment assembled, the cast gave an extraordinarily polished, near-perfect performance. The 'buzz' among those emerging from the theatre, many of them in tears, after a prolonged standing ovation, was unmistakable. Judged by the initial press reviews, however, *Les Misérables* was a flop that might never open in the West End.

# Opening Night
## and After

The Palace Theatre

After a long, emotional standing ovation on the evening of 8 October 1985, all those associated with *Les Misérables* believed they had a hit on their hands. But the first batch of critics' comments, with only a very few exceptions, ran the gamut from faint praise to scathing contempt. They were nearly all, Mackintosh, Nunn and Caird recall, 'non-selling reviews'. 'Reflecting on the uneasy week that followed the opening night, Trevor Nunn added: 'They were killers.'

Among those who reacted as enthusiastically as the first night audience itself was only a handful of critics: Michael Coveney (*Financial Times*), Sheridan Morley (*Punch*), Benedict Nightingale (*New Statesman*), the theatre critic of the *Jewish Chronicle* – a highly respected paper, but hardly a trendsetter as far as showbiz is concerned – and Sue Jameson of Independent London Radio. John Peter's review in the *Sunday Times* was good but by no means a rave review. Coveney and Morley were the two critics who immediately perceived the relationship *Les Misérables* bore to serious opera, and said so.

The negative reviewers far outnumbered this small band of supporters. VICTOR HUGO ON THE GARBAGE DUMP, headlined the influential *Observer* whose critic, Michael Ratcliffe, called it 'a witless and synthetic entertainment. Nunn and Caird', he wrote, 'have emasculated Hugo's Olympian perspective and reduced it to the trivialising and tearful aesthetic of rock opera and the French hit parade of ten (fifteen?) years ago.' In the *Sunday Telegraph*, Francis King wrote that it 'stands in the same relation to the original as a singing telegram to an epic'. 'Despite the grandeur of the music, the courage of the intentions, "Les Misérables" has, sadly, been reduced to "the Glums",' wrote Jack Tinker in the *Daily Mail*. Milton Shulman was almost equally as scathing in the *Standard*.

The BBC's influential arts programme, *Kaleidoscope*, gave *Les Misérables* a very muted welcome; 'the music by Claude-Michel Schönberg is adequate if conventional and unmemorable, the lyrics uninspiring and at times bathetic,' wrote David Kelley in the influential *Times Literary Supplement*. 'My most positive feeling about Tuesday's multi-authored adaptation of Victor Hugo's "Les Misérables" is gratitude that it drove me to read the book,' wrote Irving Wardle in *The Times*, describing the show as 'pushbutton emotionalism at the expense of character and content.'

Those against 'Les Mis' fell into two mutually contradictory categories: the first (like Ratcliffe) chided Mackintosh, Nunn and Caird for daring to reduce the monumental Victor Hugo epic masterpiece to a three and a half hour piece of musical theatre – indeed what angered Trevor Nunn most, he now recalls, was 'the hypocrisy of some theatre journalists who gave their readers the impression that Victor Hugo's novels were their favourite bedtime reading'; the second category up-braided them for tackling, as John Peter put it, 'a deeply adolescent book', and questioned 'the value of all this story-telling skill being lavished on a turgid and wobbly tale'. There was also an undercurrent of resentment that the RSC, a subsidised company, should be involved in a 'commercial' musical production.

Traditionally, Cameron Mackintosh holds a luncheon party after the opening of a new show. It was held at the Dewynter advertising agency, which handles all of Mackintosh's shows, and whose well-known theatre poster designer, Russ Eglin, had adapted the memorable 'Cosette' engraving by Emile Bayard (the illustrator of Victor Hugo's books), which had been used so effectively by Boublil and Schönberg on the cover of the original French record.

The party was more of a wake. For two days and sleepless nights, Mackintosh seriously debated whether to cut his (and his backers') losses and not attempt to transfer *Les Misérables* to the West End after its scheduled ten-week Barbican run. 'Cameron went through forty-eight hours of gloom,' Caird recalls. 'He really was knocked sideways by the adverse critical response.' The trouble was, says Mackintosh, 'I had only forty-eight hours to make the crucial decision whether to go ahead and risk losing another £300,000 – which was what the transfer from the Barbican to the Palace Theatre would cost. I had already put down a non-refundable £50,000 sum for my option on the Palace. I asked for more time, but this was refused. If I had said no, as many people wanted me to, the career of "Les Misérables", the musical, would probably have ended there and then after its Barbican Theatre run. I would have lost the possibility of the Palace Theatre – and the future of "Les Misérables" – for ever.'

In the middle of the 'party' Mackintosh called the Barbican Theatre, and found the picture was not quite as gloomy as they'd all suspected. 'I'm amazed you managed to get through,' he was told, 'the phones haven't stopped ringing. We've sold a record five thousand tickets already.' Within three days, the show was playing to capacity audiences; from then on, until the end of its Barbican run, 'Les Mis' was sold out. Public opinion clearly differed from that of most critics, and word-of-mouth did the rest.

Some two weeks later, highly favourable reviews appeared in

Alain Boublil at the Tokyo première

*Newsweek*, *Time*, the *International Herald Tribune* (Morley again), the *New York Times*, the *Washington Post* and the French weekly *L'Express* putting the earlier adverse reactions into perspective. *Newsweek* called it 'a musical that makes history'. 'Rumour has it that "Les Misérables" first opened in Paris in 1980,' said *L'Express*. 'Not so – it was born in London last October 8.' Staunch defenders of 'Les Mis' like Benedict Nightingale and Sheridan Morley, freelancers both, wrote indefatigably about the uniqueness of 'Les Mis'. 'These international reactions were our lifeline,' says Nunn. Very soon after they appeared, Cameron Mackintosh began getting enquiries from Japan and the USA about the possibility of producing *Les Misérables* abroad.

But even with all the Barbican performances sold out, the move to the West End remained a gamble. 'There was no way of imagining it would be a mega-success,' says Nunn. 'Personally, I thought it would run for three months at the Barbican and that would be that.'

The pressure on Cameron Mackintosh *not* to transfer *Les Misérables* to the West End was considerable. To understand why, one must go into the financial arrangements behind the show – and Mackintosh's relationship with Andrew Lloyd Webber and his Really Useful Group which had just bought the Palace Theatre on the corner of London's Shaftesbury Avenue and Charing Cross Road. Mackintosh's £50,000 deposit towards the rental of the Palace Theatre from December 1985 onwards was in addition to the production costs – estimated at £900,000 – which had been raised as follows: £200,000 from John Gow, a New Zealand-based backer; £200,000 from two wealthy American entrepreneurs, Karen Goodwin and Elizabeth Williams, on behalf of the huge US Mutual Benefit Insurance Company; the RSC itself put up no cash – its 'below-the-line' contribution was considered – by agreement between Cameron Mackintosh and David Brierly, the RSC Chief Executive – to be worth £300,000; and Mackintosh raised the rest of the money from his regular faithful backers.

Because of the Really Useful Group's Palace Theatre connection, Andrew Lloyd Webber's reaction to *Les Misérables* was crucial. As Mackintosh recalls, 'he clearly didn't like it'. Through third parties, Webber tried to convey the message that Mackintosh would be a 'catastrophic idiot' to continue with it. His opinion was, perhaps, not entirely disinterested: *Phantom of the Opera* was not yet in rehearsal (it was, in fact, almost a year away from its première) but Webber would have liked to have seen it open at the Palace Theatre. 'Andrew even offered to refund the deposit,' says Mackintosh.

The possibility that anyone would make a profit from *Les Misérables* seemed very remote, but with the active encouragement of his backers, Mackintosh decided to move 'Les Mis' to the Palace after all, trimming it down to just over three hours. John Caird is still slightly upset about some of the cuts. '"Little People" probably deserved it; it was too damned sentimental,' he says. 'On the eve of an insurrection in which people are going to lose their lives it was wrong to have a song about how great it is to be short. Nobody laughed and why should they? It was Artful Dodger whimsy.' Caird still regrets, however, that the original Fenton pieces for Gavroche were not included instead. If ever there is an amended English version of the show he would like to reinstate the Cosette–Valjean meeting. 'It was beautifully written — one of the most moving scenes in the show,' he says. 'It was taken out for technical reasons, but the well scene was moving and could have stayed.' There were also those who argued, to Caird's fury, that since 'Les Mis' was a family show it was wrong to include a scene apparently condoning little girls talking to strangers!

Meanwhile, night after night at the Barbican, 'Les Mis' was ending to standing ovations. One of those who rose to their feet at the end of an early performance, clapping enthusiastically, was the Princess of Wales.

Claude-Michel Schönberg during rehearsals for the original London production

Whatever Webber's personal misgivings about *Les Misérables*, he spoke to the Palace Theatre staff shortly before the show's move to ensure that the 'Les Mis' cast received a warm welcome and from December 1985 onwards, says Mackintosh, Webber's theatre has proved 'a wonderful London home'.

At the very start of the Palace Theatre run, bookings were disappointing — a mere £300,000 to start with — far less than Mackintosh had expected. Then, in a completely unforeseen way, they simply took off and the show has been sold out ever since. The test of any London show's success is in the state of booking for the matinées — the 'difficult slot' — and these too were consistently sold out. That's the way things have been ever since. As it entered its fifth year at the Palace, 'Les Mis' advance bookings remained at a near-constant figure of £2.5 million.

Another pointer towards the eventual success of 'Les Mis' was the foreign interest in the show. Early on in its Palace Theatre run, Roger Stevens came to London and decided he wanted the show for his Kennedy Center in Washington before it went to Broadway. Japanese executives from the Toho organisation saw the show and bought it. 'Les Mis' was generating its own momentum, though there was still no inkling that it would start competing in absolute terms, not only with *Cats* but with all-time favourites like *My Fair Lady*. The mythic career of *Les Misérables* had begun.

Three months into 1986, Mackintosh was on the road, preparing for the foreign 'Les Mis' productions. It was always his policy to maintain full control: in the cases of the United States and Australia, his own production companies put on *Les Misérables*; elsewhere, both with the 'reproduction' companies

The '*Les Misérables* School', Japan

and the less expensive 'non-reproduction' companies in Budapest, Tel Aviv, Reykjavik and Gdynia, he insisted on closely supervising all the artistic elements and approving all the artistic teams involved. The American version of 'Les Mis', opening at the Kennedy Center in Washington and then transferring to the Broadway Theatre in New York (a theatre belonging to the Shuberts, who had actually been lukewarm in their original response to the London show), was, in fact, a technical improvement on the Palace Theatre production. The moving barricades and the revolving stage action were computerised. Hersey also improved on the lighting (in the sewer and Javert suicide scenes) and the original New York company benefited from two of the London production's stars – Frances Ruffelle as Éponine and Colm Wilkinson himself. When America's Equity (actors' union) balked at using Wilkinson, Mackintosh, who had held extensive auditioning sessions in the States, let it be known that he would be prepared not to open at all in America if he couldn't get permission to bring the British Valjean over.

By this time, of course, the amazing success of the London production of 'Les Mis' had made American audiences impatient to see it themselves – and the critical response was overwhelmingly favourable. Now, too, plans went ahead for a Japanese version of *Les Misérables*; this was probably the greatest challenge of all.

The Toho company, Japan's large film, television and entertainment conglomerate, went about planning the show with extraordinary foresight and thoroughness. 'Musical traditions are different in Japan,' says John Caird who spent three months annually over three consecutive years co-directing the Japanese-language production. 'So are singing standards, and though musicals are not entirely unknown in Japan, their performers tend to work in one big corporate company, and their backgrounds are mostly in classical theatre and film work. We had to form an entirely new entity to provide a fund of talent from which we would later pick the cast.' A year before rehearsals began, the Toho organisation set up the '*Les Misérables* School' to teach promising candidates the art of musical theatre/rock opera. Since agents don't exist in Japan, volunteers were canvassed, advertisements appeared on campuses, in newspapers, in green rooms of existing theatres and on noticeboards of drama and opera schools. Those who auditioned to join the school, says Caird, 'were mostly kids with big strong voices who were budding actors. We trained them in movement, speech and song. It was like a rock opera version of "The Dirty Dozen". They arrived as raw recruits, some of them very unpromising material indeed. They had no idea what they were getting themselves into, and, of course, we had to attract far more people than we could actually use.'

Scenes from Japan's *Les Misérables*

In the 'actors' studio' traditions of the RSC, the Japanese cast, once established, found itself subjected to an intensive course on Christianity, radicalism and nineteenth-century European history. 'Revolution is not basically a Japanese concept,' says Caird, 'nor is there a strong Christian tradition. We had to start from absolute grass-roots.'

Language was another great problem. Though he picked up some colloquial Japanese, Caird directed through his interpreter, a remarkable lady called Mie Kakigahara. 'She's a genius,' says Caird. 'Her empathetic nature was such that she could actually complete my sentences. The structure of the Japanese language is such that you usually can't really start translating until you've heard the whole sentence. She would break down what I was saying into separate chunks, and so forceful was she that, after my departure, the cast asked her to solve directing problems. She would say, "but I'm only the interpreter." They couldn't believe it, so convincingly had she stood in for me.'

The rendering of the lyrics into Japanese also presented unusual problems. A musical score was prepared, with several lines of accompanying text. Above the piano score and the singers' musical notes were the original English lyrics. Immediately under the singers' score was the phonetic rendering in Japanese of what was being sung. Underneath that was the same Japanese text, this time in Japanese ideograms.

The Japanese lyrics presented the same problem as musical theatre in any language – they had to be singable – plus a few others. Thus Fantine's famous soliloquy 'I Dreamed a Dream' which starts:

> There was a time when men were kind
> When their voices were soft
> And their words inviting.
> There was a time when love was blind
> And the world was a song
> And the song was exciting.

became, in Japanese:

> Long ago men sweet words whispered,
> love intoxicated,
> filled were days gone by . . .
> I dream saw hope
> high-live-kite, love forever, God forgive . . .

Another feature of the Japanese production (sponsored by the Japanese perfume conglomerate Shiseido) was that it was the only one in which two major stars, Sakae Takita and Takeshi Kaga, alternated in the roles of Javert and Valjean. 'Kaga, we knew, would make a wonderful Javert but he wouldn't do it because Takita was playing the lead,' says Caird. 'I suggested they alternate, they agreed, and we had Kaga open as Valjean

# Emile Bayard (1837–1891)

Emile Bayard was Victor Hugo's favourite illustrator, famous in his own lifetime for his brilliant portraits of Fantine, Éponine, Valjean and Javert, but best known today by people all over the world for 'his' Cosette, used originally on the sleeve of the French 'Les Mis' record in 1980, and now famous as the *Les Misérables* logo.

Bayard, a prolific lithographer for magazines and books (he illustrated the works of Edmond About – then a fashionable novelist, almost as well known as Hugo himself), was one of the leaders of the nineteenth-century academic painting school, somewhat unjustly known as 'le style pompier'.

With infinite attention to detail, Emile Bayard worked for months on huge paintings, of which the best known are 'After the Battle of Waterloo' and 'Sedan 1870'. His real talent, however, lay in his abilities as a brilliant portraitist. In the tradition of the time, he also used his drawing skills to rework original sketches by explorers and travellers, sometimes even transforming photographs of exotic places into lithographs. A close friend of Honoré Daumier and cartoonists such as Paul Gavarni, Henri Monnier, Alfred Grevin, Jean-Louis Forain and Emmanuel Poiré (better known as Caran d'Ache), he wrote about their work, about spotting fakes and identifying antiques.

Quintessentially a wealthy Parisian 'society painter' with pupils and his own 'atelier', Emile Bayard showed a remarkable understanding of Victor Hugo's work as seen in his illustrations of the cast of characters in *Les Misérables*.

**THE HiLLS ARE ALIVE...**

VIENNA PREMIERE TONIGHT

**OPENS TONIGHT IN TEL AVIV**

# LES MISÉRABLES

**Premieres tonight in Gdynia, Poland**

**Liberty Belle.**

PHILADELPHIA PREMIERE TONIGHT

"We always get our Miz!"

**Opens tonight - in Toronto**

# Les Misérables

**PREMIERED LAST NIGHT IN REYKJAVIK**

**INVADING OSLO TONIGHT**

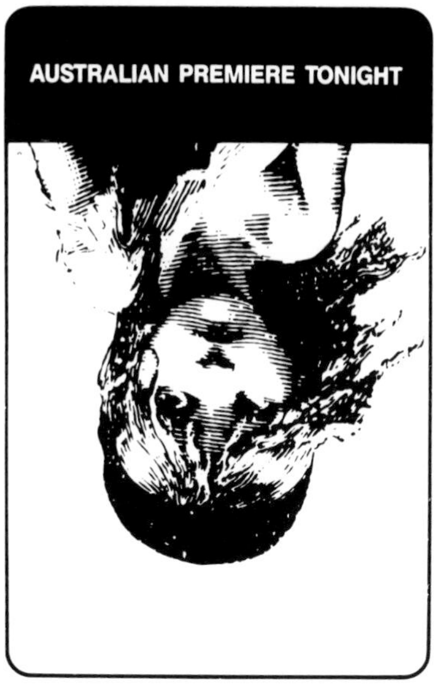

AUSTRALIAN PREMIERE TONIGHT

Hooray from Hollywood!

OPENED THIS WEEK IN LOS ANGELES AT THE SHUBERT THEATRE

for the preview and Takita playing Valjean for the Royal Opening.' Having the same person alternating in two roles meant a punishingly tough rehearsal period. 'It's impossible to have an actor rehearse two different parts on the same day,' says Caird, 'but with the Japanese cast, during rehearsal time, the problem for me was to get them to take adequate time to rest. They wanted to rehearse seventeen hours a day, including Sundays.' The Japanese cast provided other surprises: Kaho Shimada, the actress playing Éponine – who began rehearsals with no knowledge whatsoever of English – turned out to be a stunning interpreter of her part, and the Japanese Fantine, says Caird, 'is probably the best Fantine of all time – vocally heart-rending.'

Practically the entire Japanese Royal Family, with the exception of the ailing Emperor Hirohito and Empress Nagako, attended the Tokyo première and talked at length to all those involved in the production at a party afterwards. This 'royal' première was very, very different from other 'Les Mis' openings. 'Japanese audiences, we were warned, are less demonstrative,' says Caird. 'There was a little ripple of applause after some songs, and at the end the clapping was demure – it nearly died out before the stars came on – then it became more rhythmic and as the cast took bow after bow, it continued relentlessly, for at least fifteen minutes. The Toho organisation said it was the most extraordinary thing they had ever seen. It was the complete opposite to Broadway reactions, where we got an instant, crazed roaring, an immediate, almost *too* overwhelming response.'

After the double success of the London and Broadway 'Les Mis' productions, news that the show was opening in Los Angeles, at the Shubert Theatre, led to riots outside the Methodist church in West Hollywood where auditioning was to take place. 'So many people came that a ceiling was set, on a first come, first heard, basis. This system broke down when three thousand hopefuls showed up, many sleeping in their cars overnight to be sure of being on the list at opening-time. Elinore O'Connell showed up on the third day of casting at 7 a.m. to find 105 other people had got there first. As she later said, 'I completely freaked out. They slammed these double doors in front of hundreds of people. I was devastated. Everyone else complained for a few minutes and then went to lunch. Not me. I made a complete fool of myself. I sat down on the sidewalk and started to cry. I was so overwhelmed with the thought of having worked that hard to prepare and then not even getting a chance to sing for these people.' Almost twelve hours after her arrival, she went in, auditioned, was politely thanked, and left. After a series of subsequent auditions, she was chosen to play Fantine.

With the proliferation of 'Les Mis' productions across the

United States (Los Angeles, Boston, Philadelphia) and throughout the world (a pirated version was put on in Seoul during the 1988 Olympic Games), the casting process for each new show spawned a fresh wave of talent, with actors promoted from company to principal roles. The 'bus and truck' company that took 'Les Mis' to Tampa and other Florida towns beginning in December 1988 included a Fantine who had been the Los Angeles understudy for that role and a Jean Valjean (Gary Barker) was also an old 'Les Mis' hand, again having understudied the role in Los Angeles, and played it on stage eleven times. This travelling company also attracted considerable attention: *Variety* called it 'the biggest legit show on wheels', practically indistinguishable from the New York production. The *Tampa Tribune* called it 'absolutely, the best theatre on the road. This is no road-scrawny "Cats" in which Broadway's celestial junkyard-in-the-round is reduced to two lines of Christmas tree lights. Instead this "Les Mis" formidably evokes the complexity and majesty of the real thing in New York.'

Similarly, the global success of 'Les Mis' has also led to a second generation of directors: Richard Jay-Alexander, who directed the 'bus and truck' 'Les Mis' company, as well as the Toronto production, first started work on the show as associate director to Nunn and Caird on the first Washington and Broadway productions. Bob Billig, who conducted the orchestra for the initial Broadway show, became the musical supervisor for all five American companies, as well as the key musical authority responsible for the 1989 'Les Mis' symphonic concert in Australia. Other important figures involved in the realisation of the worldwide success of *Les Misérables* are Gale Edwards, a leading Australian director, who worked not only on the Sydney production but also directed the Vienna company, and Ken Caswell, who worked on the London and Oslo productions and will direct future productions in Spain, West Germany and the Netherlands.

Inevitably, all the second-generation performers are familiar with the lyrics, since the 'Les Mis' record has become a huge bestseller, and the main preoccupation of second-generation musical and stage directors like Billig and Jay-Alexander is to retain the spontaneity and freshness of the show, without insisting on turning out carbon copies of the original.

'We do have this expertise now,' says Billig. 'We teach according to a certain schedule, we've become much more efficient, it's now a crash course in "Les Mis", a musical Berlitz. But we don't cut corners.' Jay-Alexander, now Mackintosh's associate director for all the 'Les Mis' productions in the USA, insists that for all the emphasis on quality, 'every new production of "Les Mis" is different. The 'bus and truck' company was younger than any of the previous casts, and set a new standard

*Les Misérables* at theatres around the world

in road shows, in costs and size.' Now, Spanish-speaking Jay-Alexander says, his next goal is to direct a Spanish-language 'Les Mis' to be seen first in Mexico, then in Latin America. 'I think a Spanish version of "Les Mis", given the passion and fury of the Latin temperament, would be unbelievable', he says. 'Rebellion and the revolutionary spirit are very much part of their history.'

The Hungarian version of *Les Misérables* is probably – of all the foreign versions currently playing around the world – the most emotional, and certainly the most moving. To the Hungarian people, the barricades have very special, symbolic connotations: they cannot but recall the tragic 1956 Budapest uprising, crushed by Soviet tanks. However far Hungary has come since those days, it remains a searing, unforgettable landmark in her history. A similar emotional experience was felt when the Polish version of *Les Misérables* opened in June 1989 at the Muzyczny Theatre in Gdynia. Mackintosh has other long-term plans, even farther afield: greatly impressed by the talents of Filipino performers auditioning for his new venture, *Miss Saigon* (also written and composed by Boublil and Schönberg), he now intends to take *Les Misérables* to Asia, performed by an all-Asian cast.

# Les Misérables

# – Past, Present and Future

After receiving his Tony award in 1987, Claude-Michel Schönberg wryly thanked Puccini for not going ahead with *his*
planned version of *Les Misérables*, which would probably have
prevented him from tackling the theme afresh. But on stage,
and later screen, there were no such inhibitions: *Les Misérables*
became a play while the book was still hot off the presses: in
1863, a stage adaptation, written by Hugo's son Léopold-
Victor, played to packed houses in Brussels (but was banned in
France until after 1871).

The first film based on *Les Misérables* practically coincided
with the birth of the cinema industry in Europe. A silent French
movie directed by Albert Capellani was shown as early as 1906;
this was followed by US director James Stuart Blackton's *The
Galley-Slave* (1910) starring Maurice Costello as Valjean,
William Humphreys as Javert, Charles Kent, James Young,
Edith Storey and a host of other stars of silent movies. Blackton
returned to the theme in a second film in 1912, starring Henry
Krauss as Valjean and Henry Etiévant as Javert, Marie Ventura
as Fantine and, in one of her early film appearances, the famed
actress-nightclub star Mistinguett as Éponine.

Six years later (1918) another American, Frank Lloyd, made
a new US version with William Farnum as Valjean. The best,
and most well known silent film version – made in 1925 – was
French, with Gabriel Gabrio as Valjean, Sandra Milovanova as
both Fantine and Cosette, Jean Toulout as Javert and François
Rozet as Marius. This was followed by yet another US version
called *The Bishop's Candlesticks* (1929) directed by Norman
McKinnell, and that same year a silent Japanese version was
made by Tomu Uchida.

In 1933, French director Raymond Bernard made the first
*Les Misérables* talkie, with an extraordinarily fine cast including
the great stage and screen actor Harry Baur as Jean Valjean,
Charles Vanel as Javert (the only member of the cast to be still
alive at the time of the Barbican preview), Odette Florelle as
Fantine, Charles Dullin and Marguerite Moreno as the Thénardiers. This film, still regularly screened at the Paris *Cinéma-
thèque*, probably comes closest to the Mackintosh stage version.

Two years later (1935) came an equally star-studded American movie, directed by Richard Boleslawski, with Frederic

March as Valjean, Charles Laughton as a sinister, unforgettable Javert, John Beal as Marius and Sir Cedric Hardwicke as Bishop Myriel. A year later, the first known Russian version, called *Gavroche*, was released, directed by Tatiana Loukachevitch.

Other foreign productions included a Mexican *Les Misérables* in 1943 (directed by Fernando A. Rivero), an Egyptian version in 1944 (directed by Kamal Selim) and a memorable Italian version (1947) directed by Riccardo Freda, with Gino Cervi as Valjean and Valentina Cortesa as both Fantine and Cosette. Valentina Cortesa's performance in her first major film role brought her instant fame and a seven-year Hollywood contract. It was not the first time *Les Misérables* had been filmed in Italy — there had, in fact, been six previous films, none of them of great artistic value — but like Maurice Bernard's French version, this one was a landmark in the history of European cinema. This extremely expensive film included several thousand extras, and to give the barricades scenes greater realism, Freda pitched 'armies' of real-life Italian workers against squads of real-life students, some of them right-wingers. The mostly left-wing workers displayed considerable revolutionary zeal, and in the filmed mêlée, which got completely out of hand, sixty-five extras were wounded.

There was another memorable Japanese version (1950) directed by Daisuké Itoh, with the famed Japanese actor Sesue Hayakawa in the role of Jean Valjean, and Hollywood returned to *Les Misérables* in 1952 with a great director (Lewis Milestone) and some superb actors. Unaccountably, it missed the mark. With Michael Rennie as Valjean, Debra Paget as Cosette, Edmund Gwenn as Bishop Myriel, and Robert Newton unashamedly hamming it up as Javert, the film, made by Twentieth Century Fox, attracted ferocious criticism. The *Evening Standard* vented its spleen on Newton — 'mincing plump and baggy-eyed across the screen like a retired demon king, twirling invisible moustaches before every sentence . . . Michael Rennie, as a galleyslave,' the same critic added, was 'covered in false hair, clanking great chains and looked altogether like The Thing from Another World.' A southern Indian film based on *Les Misérables* was made in the Tamil language by K. Ramnoth in 1955, with the well known southern Indian actor Sohrab Modi in the role of Jean Valjean.

But the most memorable film version was yet another French one, released in 1958, directed by Jean-Paul Le Chanois. This had Jean Gabin as Valjean, Bernard Blier as Javert, Danièle Delorme as Fantine, Béatrice Altariba as Cosette, Bourvil as Thénardier, Silvia Montfort as Éponine, and the late Giani Esposito (whose film career was cut tragically short by an early death) as Marius. Serge Reggiani, another actor who achieved lasting fame, played Enjolras. This version had overt political overtones, was shot in Potsdam (East Germany) and contained some scenes that shocked purists: since the age gap between the veteran actor Gabin (Valjean) and Blier (Javert) was enormous, Le Chanois wrote in a scene where Javert, as Gabin's slave-driving custodian, points out Valjean to his son, warning him that 'here is the worst kind of prisoner, who tried to escape four times.' It is this boy who grows up to be the Javert who dogs Valjean's steps, after his release and conversion.

Every decade, it seemed, a well-known French director found a reason for trying his hand at a *Les Misérables* remake. Shortly after directing the Boublil–Schönberg musical version at the Paris Palais des Sports, Robert Hossein started work in 1981 on a mammoth television and film version (without asking Boublil or Schönberg for their collaboration). His scriptwriter was Alain Decaux, historian and later one of President François Mitterrand's cabinet ministers, in charge of promoting the French language. Their version (a four-hour television production as well as a three-hour film) was the most expensive ever, with thirty-three weeks' shooting, 3000 extras and 500 sewer rats. It cost 50 million francs, and was old-fashioned and trite in its approach to the story. It did, however, have an impressive cast, which included the late Lino Ventura as Valjean, Michel Bouquet as Javert and Jean Carmet as Thénardier.

By this time, *Les Misérables* had also been a perennial theme for several television series around the world. *The Fugitive*, the longest-running serial ever, was loosely based on the book; two British television serials and one American tried, with only limited success, to recreate the atmosphere of nineteenth-century France. Richard Jordan as Jean Valjean and Anthony Perkins as Javert somehow remained incorrigibly American throughout. There had in fact been so many film and television versions worldwide that Robert Hossein claimed Ventura to be the thirty-fifth Valjean on screen.

The highly successful international career of the Mackintosh-Boublil-Schönberg 'Les Mis' is not confined to the theatre: for Australia Day, on 26 January 1989, a free, open-air concert was staged as part of Australia's bicentennial celebrations, organised by Mackintosh and sponsored by Qantas and the Festival of Sydney. It featured an international singing cast, symphonic orchestral accompaniment, back-projections of stills and close-up monitored camerawork on stage. Over 125,000 people turned up, some of whom had slept in Domain Park all night to be sure of getting seats. A huge video screen relayed everything to those too far away to see anything on stage.

But perhaps the most adventurous, and certainly the most complicated, 'Les Mis' production was not seen by any but those directly involved in its making. This was a very special CD recording, made in London, New York, Los Angeles and Sydney with the London Philharmonic Orchestra, and members

Claude-Michel Schönberg, Cameron Mackintosh and Alain Boublil after 'Les Mis' collected seven Tony awards in 1987

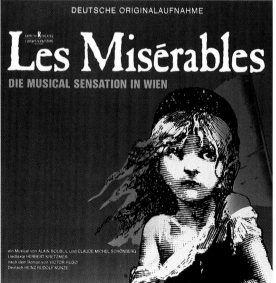

Cameron Mackintosh, Alain Boublil
and Claude-Michel Schönberg
between auditioning sessions in
Brisbane, Australia

of the New York, Sydney, Los Angeles, London and Tokyo 'Les Mis' companies. Some, like New York's Jean Valjean, Gary Morris, were able to record with the orchestra at the CTS studio in Wembley, while others, like Philip Quast (Australia's Javert) and Kaho Shimada (Japan's Éponine), were recorded in Sydney, and other company members were recorded in New York and Los Angeles. David Caddick, who produced this record and travelled around the world with tapes packed in metal cases weighing a total of 400 lbs, had the unenviable task of piecing orchestra and song recordings together, into a whole. There were additional problems: Kaho Shimada was singing in English (a language with which she was still unfamiliar) for the first time and some of the actors worked with only very basic vocal tracks. The miracle is that the result sounds as though everything was recorded at the same time and place. This CD is the only one to contain every note Schönberg wrote, with a sixty-five-strong orchestral ensemble, and a cast of seventy-five singers.

So successful was the Australian concert that others are now in preparation. Many who attend will, of course, have seen the stage version of 'Les Mis', which so far has grossed over $450 million, and many, many more own the record. Why do they keep coming? Why have some fans seen it half a dozen times or more, at different performances throughout the world? Why is the $40 million film version of the Boublil-Schönberg *Les Misérables* (with author and composer responsible for the screenplay) expected to be a massive hit when it comes out in 1992?

One reason is that *Les Misérables* tugs at our heart-strings in ways that other plays don't, affecting those who perform in it as well as those who go to see it. The cast of 'Les Mis's First National Company, for instance, playing in Boston, Washington, Philadelphia, Chicago and Detroit, found Victor Hugo's emotional 'message' so compelling that they raised money, not only for the homeless (through the Washington-based Community for Creative Non-Violence Shelter For The Homeless, CCNV, where ten members of the cast devoted one evening a week to working in a centre for the homeless), but also set aside two hundred tickets for the homeless who mingled with the more affluent members of the audience in the Kennedy Center. Afterwards, the *Washington Post* quoted 'Michael', one of the homeless (who would only allow his first name to be used) as saying, 'It reminded me of a lot of things I was going through: coming out of prison, not having a home or a job, then having someone help me like that priest'. Included in the theatre programme of the First National Company of 'Les Mis' is a letter inviting the audience to volunteer for community service and help raise funds for the homeless. 'If the story of these characters moves you,' it reads, 'you can be sure that it has the same effect on those of us who portray them night after night.'

All over America, the 'Les Mis' companies have, almost always on their own initiative, raised funds totalling over $4 million for a variety of causes, humanitarian and ecological: the London company raised money for the victims of the Lockerbie disaster just a few days after the Pan Am plane crashed in December 1988; the Australian company has set up the '*Les Misérables* Amazon Fund' to help protect the Amazon rainforest; on Broadway special 'Les Mis' posters were produced, signed by the entire cast and sold for $25 each which raised over $25,000 for the 'Equity Fights AIDS' campaign; a special performance in aid of the Actors' Fund at the Shubert Theatre in Los Angeles raised $45,000; a benefit performance for the homeless in Washington raised over $300,000; a gala performance for the New York homeless, with tickets priced from $75 to $500, also resulted in large amounts of money. Charity and benefit galas, involving Mackintosh and members of the various companies, are a regular feature of 'Les Mis' in the United States. No other play, in the history of the theatre, has generated such social concern, or raised so much money for charity.

Dudu Fisher, the Israeli Jean Valjean, was no theatre performer until he saw *Les Misérables* at the Palace Theatre in London. An Israeli cantor in great demand at bar mitzvahs, he saw the show every night of his stay in London, and returned to Tel Aviv determined, as he put it, 'either to play Jean Valjean or else emigrate to any country that would have me and would give me the chance to do so'. Fisher, a naturally gifted tenor who is to Israel what Colm Wilkinson is to Ireland, auditioned when the Tel Aviv production was in preparation, and was selected. Like Wilkinson, he claims that the part has changed his life – 'I wish I could be him in real life', he says. 'The story of "Les Misérables" is so near to us. It's about war, it's about poverty. Every night I perform, I feel the emotional wave from the audience engulfing me.'

Nothing, however, moved the various companies playing *Les Misérables* around the world as much as the Chinese pro-democracy movement of May–June 1989 with its tragic, bloody ending. Here, life reflected art with almost unbearable intensity. Letters poured in from members of the cast to the Cameron Mackintosh office in New York describing the uncanny sense of participating in a play that was also a mirror-image of reality. A letter from Dann Fink, a member of the Los Angeles 'Les Mis' company (he plays Feuilly, Enjolras's side-kick), was typical of many: 'I have never in my life', he wrote just after Chinese army tanks had crushed the students' non-violent demonstration on Tiananmen Square, 'felt a kinship with my work as strongly as I did this weekend. To witness the carnage

Cosette and the Australian '*Les Misérables* Amazon Fund'

*Washington Post*, 4 June 1989: Cosette and the legacy of Tiananmen Square

and brutality as happened in Beijing, and then to walk on stage and be part of that same event, barely two centuries removed, was at once frightening, chilling, sad, disturbing, and yet exhilarating . . . I seemed united with their cause and cries as we played out for 1800 people exactly what we had moments before been watching on TV. It was the first time I have been devastated by the timeless *reality* of "Les Mis". At least I had the opportunity to touch someone the same way the Beijing students have touched (and forever changed) me.'

The emotion was not confined to the US. Just after the Beijing massacre, Vienna's 'Les Mis' company dedicated the first performance of the newly reopened show 'to the memory of the Chinese people fighting for democracy'. After the show, marked by a minute's silence for the victims of Tiananmen Square, members of the cast took out a collection among the audience for Amnesty International, while both Cameron Mackintosh and the Viennese cast contributed their share of the day's proceeds.

Charitable causes and fund-raising apart, the very characters of *Les Misérables*, Schönberg believes, attract similar kinds of people to play them: it is quite extraordinary, he notes, how alike all the singing Éponines are in London, New York, Sydney and Tokyo, not just physically but in their thinking and their daily lives, and it is no coincidence that most of the Valjeans not only look alike, but also share many character traits. The casts of *Les Misérables*, he says, are composed of archetypes of human society: every community, every major organisation, almost any group has its Javerts, its Thénardiers and its Fantines and every one of us longs to be the kind of saint Valjean finally becomes. The universal aspect of *Les Misérables* though, has less to do with political upheavals and revolution than with the eternal truths about human nature – and belief in God. In essence, the story of Jean Valjean is that of a sudden, Pauline conversion, and a determination to retain the almost impossible ethical standards he has set himself. The quest for saintliness is the one thing all religions have in common.

Though not all countries have directly experienced revolution, barricades or insurgencies, we can all identify with the social injustice *Les Misérables* condemns and we all aspire to the perfect world Victor Hugo hoped time would usher in. The memories of the dead linger in any society, in any family: we all feel guilt at one time or another for surviving adversity, disease or war, while others less lucky have perished. What the show demonstrates, to haunting, memorable words and music, is that we are all, in short, part of the *Les Misérables* family – the family of humankind.

# *Opening Nights*

| | |
|---|---|
| 18 September 1980 | Original arena version of *Les Misérables* at the Palais des Sports, Paris |
| 8 October 1985 | Barbican Theatre, London |
| 4 December 1985 | Palace Theatre, London |
| 27 December 1986 | Opera House, Kennedy Center, Washington DC |
| 12 March 1987 | Broadway Theatre, New York |
| 17 July 1987 | Imperial Theatre, Tokyo |
| 9 August 1987 | Cameri Theatre, Tel Aviv |
| 14 August 1987 | Rock Theatre, Szeged, Hungary |
| 14 September 1987 | Rock Theatre, Vigzinhaz, Budapest |
| 27 November 1987 | Theatre Royal, Sydney |
| 15 December 1987 | Shubert Theatre, Boston |
| 26 December 1987 | National Theatre of Iceland, Reykjavik |
| 17 March 1988 | Det Norske Teatret, Oslo |
| 25 March 1988 | Chunichi Theatre, Nagoya |
| 9 April 1988 | Umeda-Koma Theatre, Osaka |
| 1 June 1988 | Shubert Theatre, Los Angeles |
| 15 September 1988 | Raimund Theatre, Vienna |
| 27 October 1988 | Forest Theatre, Philadelphia |
| 20 November 1988 | Bus and Truck tour opens in Tampa, Florida, thereafter Miami; Orlando; St Petersburg; Atlanta; Kansas City; St Louis; Columbus; Grand Rapids; Cincinnati; East Lansing; Bloomington; Louisville; Nashville; Birmingham; Jacksonville; New Orleans; Houston; Memphis; Dallas; Pittsburgh; Cleveland; St Paul; Denver; Iowa City; Urbana; Des Moines; Champaign; Schenectady; Syracuse; Providence; New Haven; Hartford; Scranton; Rochester; Buffalo; Indianapolis; Knoxville; Norfolk; Richmond; Raleigh; Charlotte; Clearwater |
| 15 March 1989 | Royal Alexander Theatre, Toronto |
| 25 March 1989 | Auditorium Theatre, Chicago |
| 30 June 1989 | Theatre Muzyczny, Gdynia |
| 13 September 1989 | Fisher Theatre, Detroit |
| 28 October 1989 | Princess Theatre, Melbourne |
| 1 November 1989 | Curren Theatre, San Francisco |
| 10 January 1990 | Mechanic Theatre, Baltimore |
| 22 March 1990 | Shubert Theatre, Boston |
| 13 June 1990 | S Alberta Jubilee Centre, Calgary |
| 12 July 1990 | National Theatre, Washington |
| 12 September 1990 | Cirkus Theater, Stockholm |
| 17 October 1990 | His Majesty's Theatre, Perth |
| 25 October 1990 | Forrest Theatre, Philadelphia |
| 1 January 1991 | Festival Theatre, Adelaide |
| 24 January 1991 | Theatre St Denis, Montreal |
| 28 February 1991 | Theater Carré, Amsterdam |
| 9 March 1991 | Lyric Theatre, Brisbane |
| 20 April 1991 | Odense Teater, Odense |
| 29 May 1991 | ACTEA Theatre, Auckland, New Zealand |
| 6 December 1991 | Circustheater, Scheveningen |
| 14 April 1992 | Palace Theatre, Manchester |
| 25 June 1992 | Vinorhady Theatre, Prague |
| 16 September 1992 | Nuevo Apolo, Madrid |
| 27 December 1992 | Ostregaswerks, Copenhagen |
| Productions under Discussion | Barcelona, Berlin, Buenos Aires, Cape Town, Dublin, Durban, Estonia, Hamburg, Johannesburg, Mexico, Moscow, Munich, Peru, Rio de Janeiro, Rome, San Paulo, Sofia. |

# *Recordings*

'Les Misérables' – Original French concept album (Album, cassette and CD)
P 1980 Editions Musicales Alain Boublil Disques TREMA 2 x RC 230 310086/76 CD 710217   1980
Awarded Gold Disc, 1980

'La Faute À Voltaire' Fabrice Bernard and 'Rouge et Noir' the Company (Single)
P 1980 Editions Musicales Alain Boublil Disques TREMA RC 110 2410151 and 2548013   1980

'L'Air de la Misère' Rose Laurens (Single)
P 1980 Editions Musicales Alain Boublil Disques WEA Filipacchi
WE 101 11603 1980

'Highlights of *Les Misérables*' Compilation from the French Concept Album
P 1980 Editions Musicales Alain Boublil 1st Night Records Scene 2   1985

'I Dreamed a Dream' Rose Laurens (Maxi Single)
P 1980 Editions Musicales Alain Boublil 'I Dreamed a Dream' Patti LuPone 'Who Am I?' Colm Wilkinson 'Act One, Finale'
the Company 1st Night Records P 1985   Exallshow Ltd Score Lt   1985

'Les Misérables' – Original French concept album (Album, cassette and CD)
Re-released in United States and Canada only P 1980 Editions Musicales Alain
Boublil Relativity 88561-8247-2   1988

'Les Misérables' – London cast recording (Double album, cassette and CD)
1st Night Records P 1985 Exallshow Ltd Encore 1 Encore C1 Encore CD1   1985
Awarded Silver Disc May 1986   Gold Disc September 1986   Platinum Disc May 1988

'I Dreamed a Dream' and 'One Day More' Patti LuPone and the Company (Single)
1st Night Records P 1985 Exallshow Ltd Score 1   1985

'On My Own' Frances Ruffelle (Single)
'Do You Hear the People Sing?' the Company
P 1985 Exallshow Ltd 1st Night Records Score C2   1985

'On My Own' Frances Ruffelle, 'I Dreamed a Dream' Patti LuPone 'Do You Hear the People
Sing?' Ensemble 'Prologue' Colm Wilkinson, Roger Allam and the Ensemble (Cassette)
P 1985 Exallshow Ltd 1st Night Records Score C2   1986

'Bring Him Home' Colm Wilkinson (Single)
P 1985 Exallshow Ltd 1st Night Records Score 7   1986

'Les Misérables' – Broadway cast recording (Double Album, cassette and CD)
Geffen Records P 1987 GHS 24151, M5G 24151   1987
Awarded Gold Disc March 1989

'Les Misérables' – Japanese cast recording 'On My Own' and 'Do You Hear the People Sing?'
(Single and cassette)
Pony Canyon 7A0704, 10P3093   1987

'Les Misérables' – Israel cast recording (Album)
Hed Arzi Ltd ACUM Can 15292   1987

'Les Misérables' – Hungarian cast recording (Album)
P. Radioton 1988 SLPM 14111-B   1988

'Les Misérables' – Vienna cast recording
P Polydor GmbH 1988, 2LP 837770-1, 2CD 837770-2, 2MC 837770-4   1988

'I Dreamed a Dream' and 'Bring Him Home' Sona Macdonald and Reinhard Brussmann (Single)
P Polydor GmbH   1988

'Les Misérables' – The Complete Symphonic Recording
1st Night Records, P & C 1988 Exallshow Ltd
MIZ 1, MIZ C1, MIZ CD1   1988

'Les Misérables' – Stockholm cast recording
CBS Records LP 467870-1, CD 467870-2, MC 467870-3   1990

'Les Misérables' – Amsterdam cast recording
Phonogram bv Mercury CD 848-598-2, MC 848-598-4

'Les Misérables' – French cast recording
TREMA 1991, 2LP 310 369/370 PM 524, 2CD 710 369/370 PM 541, 2MC 110 369/370 PM 427

'Les Misérables' – Czech cast recording
Bonton Records   1992

# *Awards*

| | |
|---|---|
| **LONDON** | Best Musical Award 1986 from the London Critics Circle<br>Best Actress in a Musical (Patti LuPone) OLIVIER AWARDS<br><br>Silver, Gold and Platinum Discs |
| **NEW YORK** | EIGHT TONY AWARDS – Broadway Production<br><br>Best Musical<br>Best Book (Alain Boublil and Claude-Michel Schönberg)<br>Best Score (Alain Boublil, Claude-Michel Schönberg and Herbert Kretzmer)<br>Best Director (Trevor Nunn and John Caird)<br>Best Featured Actress in a Musical (Frances Ruffelle)<br>Best Featured Actor in a Musical (Michael Maguire)<br>Best Set Design (John Napier)<br>Best Lighting Design (David Hersey)<br><br>NEW YORK DRAMA CRITICS AWARD<br><br>Best Musical<br><br>OUTER CRITICS CIRCLE AWARD<br><br>Best Musical<br><br>FIVE DRAMA DESK AWARDS<br><br>Best Musical<br>Best Featured Actor (Michael Maguire)<br>Best Orchestrations (John Cameron)<br>Best Music (Claude-Michel Schönberg)<br>Best Set Design (John Napier)<br><br>GRAMMY<br><br>Best Original Broadway Cast Recording |
| **WASHINGTON** | HELEN HAYES AWARDS (Washington Theatre Awards Society)<br><br>Best Non-Resident Production<br>Best Actor in a Non-Resident Production (Colm Wilkinson)<br>Best Supporting Performer in a Non-Resident Production (Frances Ruffelle) |
| **LOS ANGELES** | DRAMA-LOGUE<br><br>1988 Drama-logue Publisher/Critics award to Cameron Mackintosh<br><br>THE LOS ANGELES DRAMA CRITICS CIRCLE AWARDS<br><br>Costume Design (Andreane Neofitou)<br>Lighting Design (David Hersey)<br>Original Music (Claude-Michel Schönberg) |
| **JAPAN** | Artistic Festival Prize 1987 awarded by the Agency for Cultural Affairs in Japan |
| **STOCKHOLM** | THE GULD MASKEN (GOLD MASK) AWARDS<br><br>Best Male Leading Role (Tommy Korberg)<br>Best Female Leading Role (Maria Rydberg)<br>Best Male Supporting Role (Claes Malmberg)<br>The Jury's Special Prize (Ture Rangstrom) |

**AUSTRALIA** SYDNEY MO AWARDS

Best Female Performer in a Leading Role (Marina Prior)
Best Male Performer in a Leading Role (Rob Guest)
Best Female Performer in a Supporting Role (Robyn Arthur)
Best Male Performer in a Supporting Role (Anthony Warlow)

MELBOURNE GREEN ROOM AWARDS

Best Female Musical Theatre Performer (Marina Prior)
Best Male Musical Theatre Performer (Anthony Warlow)
Best Supporting Female Musical Theatre Performer (Christa Leahman)
Musical Theatre Performer of the Year (Anthony Warlow)

MUSIC CRITICS CIRCLE AWARDS

Best Musical
Best Actor of the Year in a Musical (Philip Cross)

**PARIS** THE MOLIERE AWARD

Best Musical

# Libretto

# ACT ONE

---

## PROLOGUE

*(A Chain Gang works in scorching sun)*

WORK SONG Look down, look down,
Don't look 'em in the eye.
Look down, look down,
You're here until you die.

CONVICT 1 The sun is strong
It's hot as hell below

CHORUS Look down, look down,
There's twenty years to go.

CONVICT 2 I've done no wrong,
Sweet Jesus, hear my prayer.

CHORUS Look down, look down,
Sweet Jesus doesn't care.

CONVICT 3 I know she'll wait,
I know that she'll be true.

CHORUS Look down, look down,
They've all forgotten you.

CONVICT 4 When I get free
You won't see me
'Ere for dust.

CHORUS Look down, look down,
Don't look 'em in the eye.

CONVICT 5 How long, O Lord,
Before you let me die?

CHORUS Look down, look down,
You'll always be a slave.
Look down, look down,
You're standing in your grave.

JAVERT Now bring me prisoner 24601:
Your time is up
And your parole's begun,
You know what that means.

VALJEAN Yes, it means I'm free.

JAVERT No. It means you get
Your yellow ticket-of-leave,
You are a thief.

VALJEAN I stole a loaf of bread.

JAVERT You robbed a house.

VALJEAN I broke a window pane.
My sister's child was close to death
And we were starving.

JAVERT You will starve again
Unless you learn the meaning of the law.

VALJEAN I know the meaning of those 19 years,
A slave of the law.

JAVERT Five years for what you did,
The rest because you tried to run,
Yes, 24601.

VALJEAN My name is Jean Valjean.

JAVERT And I'm Javert,
Do not forget my name.
Do not forget me
24601.

CHORUS Look down, look down,
You'll always be a slave.
Look down, look down,
You're standing in your grave.

VALJEAN Freedom is mine. The earth is still.
I feel the wind. I breathe again
And the sky clears,
The world is waking.
Drink from the pool. How clean the taste.
Never forget the years, the waste.
Nor forgive them
For what they've done.
They are the guilty – everyone.
The day begins . . .
And now let's see
What this new world
Will do for me!

FARMER You'll have to go.
I'll pay you off for the day.
Collect your bits and pieces there
And be on your way.

VALJEAN You have given me half
What the other men get –
This handful of tin
Wouldn't buy my sweat!

LABOURER You broke the law,
It's there for people to see –
Why should you get the same
As honest men like me?

VALJEAN Now every door is closed to me.
Another jail. Another key. Another chain.
For when I come to any town
They check my papers
And they find the mark of Cain.
In their eyes
I see their fear:
'We do not want you here'.

INNKEEPER'S WIFE My rooms are full
And I've no supper to spare.
I'd like to help a stranger
All we want is to be fair.

VALJEAN I will pay in advance,
I can sleep in a barn.
You see how dark it is.
I'm not some kind of dog.

INNKEEPER You leave my house!
Or feel the weight of my rod.
We're law-abiding people here,
Thanks be to God.

VALJEAN And now I know how freedom feels,
The jailer always at your heels
It is the law!
This piece of paper in my hand
That makes me cursed throughout the land
It is the law!
Like a cur
I walk the street,
The dirt beneath their feet . . .

BISHOP Come in, Sir, for you are weary,
And the night is cold out there.
Though our lives are very humble
What we have, we have to share.
There is wine here to revive you.
There is bread to make you strong.
There's a bed to rest 'til morning.
Rest from pain, and rest from wrong.

VALJEAN He let me eat my fill.
I had the lion's share.
The silver in my hand
Cost twice what I had earned
In all those nineteen years –
That lifetime of despair –
And yet he trusted me,
The old fool trusted me.
He'd done his bit of good,
I played the grateful serf
And thanked him like I should.
But when the house was still,
I got up in the night.
Took the silver,
Took my flight!

TWO CONSTABLES
1 Tell His Reverence your story.
2 Let us see if he's impressed.
1 You were lodging here last night.
2 You were the honest Bishop's guest.
  And then, out of Christian goodness.
  When he learned about your plight
1 You maintain he made a present of this silver.

BISHOP That is right.
But my friend, you left so early
Surely something slipped your mind

(BISHOP *gives* VALJEAN *two silver candlesticks*)

You forgot I gave these also –
Would you leave the best behind?
So, Messieurs, you may release him,
For this man has spoken true.
I commend you for duty
And God's blessing go with you.

(CONSTABLES *leave.* BISHOP *addresses* VALJEAN)

BISHOP But remember this, my brother:
See in this some higher plan.
You must use this precious silver
To become an honest man.
By the witness of the martyrs,
By the Passion and the Blood,
God has raised you out of darkness
I have bought your soul for God!

VALJEAN What have I done?
Sweet Jesus, what have I done?
Become a thief in the night!
Become a dog on the run!
And have I fallen so far,
And is the hour so late
That nothing remains but the cry of my hate,
The cries in the dark that nobody hears
Here where I stand at the turning of the years?

If there's another way to go
I missed it twenty long years ago.
My life was a war that could never be won,
They gave me a number and murdered Valjean.
When they chained me and left me for dead
Just for stealing a mouthful of bread.

Yet why did I allow this man
To touch my soul and teach me love?
He treated me like any other.
He gave me his trust.
He called me Brother.
My life he claims for God above.
Can such things be?
For I had come to hate the world.
This world that always hated me!

Take an eye for an eye.
Turn your heart into stone.
This is all I have lived for.
This is all I have known.
One word from him and I'd be back
Beneath the lash, upon the rack.
Instead he offers me my freedom.
I feel my shame inside me like a knife.
He told me that I have a soul.
How does he know?
What spirit comes to move my life?
Is there another way to go?

I am reaching, but I fall,
And the night is closing in,
And I stare into the void –
To the whirlpool of my sin.
I'll escape now from the world
From the world of Jean Valjean.
Jean Valjean is nothing now.
Another story must begin.

(VALJEAN *tears up yellow ticket of leave*)

## 2. *The Factory at Montreuil*

THE POOR At the end of the day you're another day
older,
And that's all you can say for the life of the poor.
It's a struggle, it's a war
And there's nothing that anyone's giving,
One more day standing about
What is it for –
One day less to be living.

At the end of the day you're another day colder
And the shirt on your back doesn't keep out the chill,
And the righteous hurry past,
They don't hear the little ones crying,
And the winter is coming on fast
Ready to kill –
One day nearer to dying.

At the end of the day there's another day dawning,
And the sun in the morning is waiting to rise –
Like the waves crash on the sand,
Like a storm that'll break any second.
There's a hunger in the land,
There's a reckoning still to be reckoned and
There's gonna be hell to pay
At the end of the day!

FOREMAN At the end of the day you get nothing for
nothing,
Sitting flat on your butt doesn't buy any bread.

WORKER 1 There are children back at home.

WORKERS 1 & 2 And the children have got to be fed.

WORKER 2 And you're lucky to be in a job.

WOMAN And in a bed.

WORKERS And we're counting our blessings!

VARIOUS WOMEN
GIRL 2 Have you seen how the foreman is fuming
today,
With his terrible breath and his wandering
hands?
GIRL 3 It's because little Fantine won't give him his
way.
GIRL 1 Take a look at his trousers, you see where he
stands!
GIRL 4 And the boss, he never knows
That the foreman is always in heat.
GIRL 3 If Fantine doesn't look out –
Watch how she goes –
She'll be out on the street!

WORKERS At the end of the day it's another day over,
With enough in your pocket to last for a week.
Pay the landlord, pay the shop,
Keep on grafting as long as you're able,
Keep on grafting till you drop
Or it's back to the crumbs off the table.
You've got to pay your way
At the end of the day.

(A GIRL *grabs a letter from* FANTINE)

GIRL And what have we here, little innocent sister?
Come on, Fantine, let's have all the news!
(*reads*) 'Ooh . . . dear Fantine, you must send us more
money . . . your child needs a doctor . . . there's no
time to lose . . .'

FANTINE Give that letter to me.
It is none of your business,
With a husband at home
And a bit on the side!
Is there anyone here
Who can swear before God
She has nothing to fear?
She has nothing to hide?

(*There follows a fight over possession of the letter*)

VALJEAN Will someone tear these two apart –
What is this fighting all about?
This is a factory, not a circus.
Now, come on ladies, settle down.
I run a business of repute,
I am the Mayor of this town
(*to* FOREMAN)
I look to you to sort this out
And be as patient as you can.

(VALJEAN *exits*)

FOREMAN Now someone say how this began!

GIRL At the end of the day
She's the one who began it!
There's a kid that she's hiding

In some little town.
There's a man she has to pay –
You can guess how she picks up the extra.
You can bet she's earning her keep
Sleeping around,
And the boss wouldn't like it!

FANTINE Yes it's true there's a child,
And the child is my daughter,
And her father abandoned us
Leaving us flat.
Now she lives with an innkeeper man
And his wife,
And I pay for the child,
What's the matter with that?

WOMEN WORKERS At the end of the day
She'll be nothing but trouble.
And there's trouble for all
When there's trouble for one!
While we're earning our daily bread,
She's the one with her hands in the butter.
You must send the slut away
Or we're all gonna end in the gutter,
And it's us who'll have to pay
At the end of the day!

FOREMAN I might have known the bitch could bite.
I might have known the cat had claws.
I might have guessed your little secret.
Ah yes, the virtuous Fantine
Who keeps herself so pure and clean.
You'd be the cause, I had no doubt
Of any trouble hereabout.
You play a virgin in the light
But need no urgin' in the night!

GIRL She's been laughing at you
While she's having her men.

WOMEN She'll be nothing but trouble again and again.

WOMAN You must sack her today.

ALL WORKERS Sack the girl today.

FOREMAN Right, my girl. On your way.

(FANTINE *is left alone*)

FANTINE There was a time when men were kind,
When their voices were soft
And their words inviting.
There was a time when love was blind
And the world was a song
And the song was exciting.
There was a time.
Then it all went wrong.

I dreamed a dream in time gone by,
When hope was high
And life worth living.
I dreamed that love would never die,
I dreamed that God would be forgiving.

Then I was young and unafraid
And dreams were made and used
And wasted.
There was no ransom to be paid,
No song unsung
No wine untasted.

But the tigers come at night
With their voices soft as thunder,
As they tear your hope apart,
As they turn your dream to shame.
He slept a summer by my side.
He filled my days
With endless wonder.
He took my childhood in his stride,
But he was gone when autumn came.

And still I dream he'll come to me,
That we will live the years together.
But there are dreams that cannot be,
And there are storms
We cannot weather . . .

I had a dream my life would be
So different from this hell I'm living,
So different now from what it seemed.
Now life has killed
The dream I dreamed.

## 3. *The Red Light District*

SAILORS

SAILOR 1 I smell women,
    Smell 'em in the air.
    Think I'll drop my anchor
    In that harbour over there.
SAILOR 2 Lovely ladies,
    Smell 'em through the smoke.
    Seven days at sea
    Can make you hungry for a poke.
SAILOR 3 Even stokers need a little stoke.

WOMEN Lovely ladies
Waiting for a bite,
Waiting for the customers
Who only come at night.
Lovely ladies
Ready for the call,
Standing up or lying down
Or any way at all.
Bargain prices up against the wall.

OLD WOMAN Come here, my dear,
Let's see this trinket you wear
This bagatelle . . .

FANTINE Madame, I'll sell it to you!

OLD WOMAN I'll give you four.

FANTINE That wouldn't pay for the chain.

OLD WOMAN I'll give you five. You're far too eager to
  sell.
It's up to you.

FANTINE It's all I have

OLD WOMAN That's not my fault.

FANTINE Please make it ten.

OLD WOMAN No more than five.
My dear, we all must stay alive.

WOMEN
ALL    Lovely ladies
    Waiting in the dark,

Ready for a thick one
Or a quick one in the park.
WHORE 1 Long time, short time,
Anytime, my dear.
Cost a little extra if you want to take all year.
ALL Quick and cheap is underneath the pier!

CRONE What pretty hair!
What pretty locks you got there.
What luck you got. It's worth a centime, my dear.
I'll take the lot.

FANTINE Don't touch me. Leave me alone.

CRONE Let's make a price. I'll give you all ten francs,
just think of that!

FANTINE (*aside*) It pays a debt.

CRONE Just think of that.

FANTINE What can I do? It pays a debt.
Ten francs may save my poor Cosette.

SAILORS

| SAILORS | WOMEN |
|---|---|
| SAILOR 3 Lovely lady! | Lovely ladies, |
| Fastest on the street – | Lovely little girls. |
| Wasn't there three minutes | |
| She was back upon her feet. | Lovely ladies, Lovely little ladies. |
| SAILOR 1 Lovely lady! | Lovely girlies, |
| What yer waiting for? | Lovely little girls. |
| Doesn't take a lot of savvy | We are lovely, lovely girls. |
| Just to be a whore. | Lovely ladies, |
| Come on, lady. | What's a lady for? |
| What's a lady *for*? | |

PIMP Gimme the dirt,
Who's that bit over there?

WHORE 1 A bit of skirt,
She's the one sold her hair.

WHORE 2 She's got a kid,
Sends her all that she can.

PIMP I might've known
There is always some man.
Lovely lady, come along and join us.
Lovely lady!

WHORE 1 Come on, dearie, why all the fuss?
You're no grander than the rest of us.
Life has dropped you at the bottom of the heap.
Join your sisters.

WHORE 2 Make money in your sleep!

WHORE 1 That's right, dearie,
Let 'im have the lot.

WHORE 3 That's right, dearie,
Show him what you've got!

WOMEN Old men, young men, take 'em as they come,
Harbour rats and alley cats and every kind of scum.
Poor men, rich men, leaders of the land.
See them with their trousers off they're never quite as
  grand.
All it takes is money in your hand.

Lovely ladies,
Going for a song.
Got a lot of callers
But they never stay for long.

FANTINE Come on, Captain, you can wear your shoes.
Don't it make a change
To have a girl who can't refuse?
Easy money
Lying on a bed.
Just as well they never see the hate
That's in your head!
Don't they know
They're making love to one already dead?

BAMATABOIS Here's something new. I think I'll give it
  a try.
Come closer, you!
I like to see what I buy . . .
The usual price
For just a slice of your pie.

FANTINE I don't want you. No, no, M'sieur, let me go.

BAMATABOIS Is this a trick? I won't pay more!

FANTINE No, not at all.

BAMATABOIS You got some nerve, you little whore,
You've got some gall.
It's the same with a tart
As it is with a grocer –
The customer sees what he gets in advance.
It's not for the whore to say 'yes sir' or 'no sir'.
It's not for the harlot to pick and to choose
Or to lead me a dance!

FANTINE I'll kill you, you bastard,
Try any of that!
Even a whore who has gone to the bad
Won't be had by a rat.

BAMATABOIS By Christ, you'll pay for what you've
  done.
This rat will make you bleed you'll see!
I guarantee, I'll make you suffer
For this disturbance of the peace,
For this insult to life and property!

FANTINE I beg you, don't report me, sir
I'll do whatever you may want . . .

BAMATABOIS Make your excuse to the police!

JAVERT Tell me quickly what's the story?
Who saw what, and why, and where?
Let him give a full description.
Let him answer to Javert!
In this nest of whores and vipers
Let one speak who saw it all.
Who laid hands on this good man here?
What's the substance of this brawl?

BAMATABOIS Javert, would you believe it –
I was crossing from the park
When this prostitute attacked me,
You can see she left her mark.

JAVERT She will answer for her actions
When you make a full report.
You may rest assured, M'sieur
That she will answer to the court.

FANTINE There's a child who sorely needs me.
Please, M'sieur, she's but 'that high'.
Holy God, is there no mercy?
If I go to jail she'll die!

JAVERT I have heard such protestations
Every day for twenty years.
Let's have no more explanations.
Save your breath and save your tears.
'Honest work. Just reward. That's the way to please the
  Lord.'

VALJEAN A moment of your time, Javert.
I do believe this woman's tale.

JAVERT But, M'sieur Mayor!

VALJEAN You've done your duty. Let her be
She needs a doctor not a gaol.

JAVERT But, M'sieur Mayor

FANTINE Can this be?

VALJEAN Where will she end –
This child without a friend?
(*to* FANTINE)
I've seen your face before –
Show me some way to help you.
How have you come to grief
In such a place as this?

FANTINE M'sieur, don't mock me now, I pray.
It's hard enough I've lost my pride!
You let your foreman send me away,
Yes, you were there
And turned aside.
I never did no wrong!

VALJEAN Is it true, what I've done?

FANTINE My daughter's close to dying . . .

VALJEAN To an innocent soul?

FANTINE If there's a God above,

VALJEAN Had I only known then . . .

FANTINE He'd let me die instead.

VALJEAN In His name my task has just begun. I will
  see it done.
I will see it done.

JAVERT But, M'sieur Mayor!

VALJEAN I will see it done!

JAVERT But, M'sieur Mayor!

VOICES Look out!
It's a runaway cart!

(*A* MAN *is pinned down by a runaway cart*)

VOICES Look at that! Look at that!
It's Monsieur Fauchelevent!
Don't approach!
Don't go near!
At the risk of your life!
He is caught by the wheel!
Oh, the pitiful man!
Stay away, turn away!
There is nothing to do!
There is nothing to do!

VALJEAN Is there anyone here
Who will rescue the man?
Who will help me to shoulder
The weight of the cart?

VOICES Don't go near him, Mr Mayor –
The load is as heavy as hell.
The old man's a goner for sure.
It'll kill you as well.

FAUCHELEVENT M'sieur le Mayor, I have no words,
You come from God, you are a saint.

JAVERT Can this be true?
I don't believe what I see!
A man your age
To be as strong as you are!
A mem'ry stirs . . .
You make me think of a man
From years ago –
A man who broke his parole.
He disappeared.
Forgive me, sir,
I would not dare . . .

VALJEAN Say what you must,
Don't leave it there . . .

JAVERT I have only known one other
Who can do what you have done.
He's a convict from the chain gang,
He's been ten years on the run.
But he couldn't run forever,
We have found his hideaway
And he's just been re-arrested,
And he comes to court today.
Well, of course, he now denies it –
You'd expect that of a 'con'.
But he couldn't run forever –
No, not even Jean Valjean!

VALJEAN You say this man denies it all
And gives no sign of understanding or repentance?

You say this man is going to trial
And that he's sure to be returned
To serve his sentence?

Come to that, can you be sure
That I am not your man?

JAVERT I have known the thief for ages
Tracked him down through thick and thin.
And to make the matter certain
There's the brand upon his skin.
He will bend. He will break.
This time there is no mistake!

## 4. The Trial

VALJEAN He thinks that man is me
He knew him at a glance!
That stranger he has found
This man could be my chance!

Why should I save his hide?
Why should I right this wrong
When I have come so far
And struggled for so long?

If I speak, I am condemned.
If I stay silent, I am damned!

I am the master of hundreds of workers.
They all look to me.
Can I abandon them?
How would they live
If I am not free?

If I speak, I am condemned
If I stay silent, I am damned!

Who am I?
Can I condemn this man to slavery?
Pretend I do not see his agony?
This innocent who bears my face
Who goes to judgment in my place.
Who am I?
Can I conceal myself for evermore?
Pretend I'm not the man I was before?
And must my name until I die
Be no more than an alibi?
Must I lie?
How can I ever face my fellow men?
How can I ever face myself again?
My soul belongs to God, I know
I made that bargain long ago
He gave me hope when hope was gone
He gave me strength to journey on
Who am I? Who am I?
I am Jean Valjean!

And so, Javert, you see it's true
That man bears no more guilt than you!

Who am I?
24601!
If you need me, I will be at the hospital.

## 5. The Hospital

(FANTINE *is so ill now that she is in a kind of delirium.*
*She imagines she can see her child at play*)

FANTINE Cosette, it's turned so cold.
Cosette, it's past your bed time!
You've played the day away,
And soon it will be night.

Come to me, Cosette, the light is fading.
Don't you see the evening star appearing?
Come to me and rest against my shoulder –
How fast the minutes fly away and every minute colder.
Hurry near, another day is dying.
Don't you hear the winter wind is crying?
There's a darkness which comes without a warning
But I will sing you lullabies and wake you in the
    morning.

(VALJEAN *enters*)

VALJEAN Oh, Fantine, our time is running out,
But, Fantine, I swear this on my life

FANTINE Look, M'sieur, where all the children play.

VALJEAN Be at peace, be at peace ever more.

FANTINE My Cosette . . .

VALJEAN Shall live in my protection.

FANTINE Take her now.

VALJEAN Your child will want for nothing.

FANTINE Good M'sieur, you come from God in
    heaven.

VALJEAN And none will ever harm Cosette
As long as I am living.

FANTINE Take my hand
The night grows ever colder

VALJEAN Then I will keep you warm.

FANTINE Take my child –
I give her to your keeping.

VALJEAN Take shelter from the storm.

FANTINE For God's sake, please stay till I am sleeping
And tell Cosette I love her.
And I'll see her when I wake . . .

(FANTINE *dies*)

JAVERT Valjean, at last,
We see each other plain!
'M'sieur le Mayor',
You'll wear a different chain!

VALJEAN Before you say another word, Javert,
Before you chain me up like a slave again.
Listen to me. There is something I must do.
This woman leaves behind a suffering child.
There is none but me who can intercede.
In Mercy's name, three days are all I need.
Then I'll return. I pledge my word.
Then I'll return . . .

JAVERT You must think me mad!
I've hunted you across the years.
Men like you can never change.
A man such as you.

VALJEAN                          JAVERT
Believe of me what you will!     (*in counterpoint*)
There is a duty that I'm sworn to do.
You know nothing of my life –
All I did was steal some bread.
You know nothing of the world –
You would sooner see me dead.
But not before I see this justice done.
I am warning you, Javert,
I'm a stronger man by far.
There is power in me yet,
My race is not yet run.
I am warning you, Javert,
There is nothing I won't dare,
If I have to kill you here.

JAVERT                          VALJEAN
Men like me can never change.    (*in counterpoint*)
Men like you can never change.
No. 24601,
My duty's to the law.
You can have no rights,
Come with me, 24601.
Now the wheel has turned around,
Jean Valjean is nothing now.
Dare you talk to me of crime
And the price you had to pay?
Every man is born in sin,
Every man must choose his way.
You know nothing of Javert.
I was born inside a gaol.
I was born with scum like you,
I am from the gutter too.

(VALJEAN *breaks a chair and threatens*)

VALJEAN And this I swear to you tonight . . .

JAVERT There is no place for you to hide.

VALJEAN Your child will live within my care.

JAVERT Wherever you may hide away.

VALJEAN And I will raise her to the light.

VALJEAN & JAVERT I swear to you, I will be there!

(VALJEAN *and* JAVERT *fight*. VALJEAN *knocks* JAVERT *out and escapes*)

## 6. *The Inn*

YOUNG COSETTE There is a castle on a cloud;
I like to go there in my sleep.
Aren't any floors for me to sweep,
Not in my castle on a cloud.

There is a room that's full of toys.
There are a hundred boys and girls.
Nobody shouts or talks too loud,
Not in my castle on a cloud.

There is a lady all in white,
Holds me and sings a lullaby.
She's nice to see
And she's soft to touch.
She says: 'Cosette, I love you very much.'

I know a place where no one's lost.
I know a place where no one cries.
Crying at all is not allowed,
Not in my castle on a cloud.

Oh help! I think I hear them now, and I'm nowhere
  near finished sweeping and scrubbing and polishing
  the floor. Oh, it's her! It's Madame!

(*Enter* MME THENARDIER *at a rush*)

MME THENARDIER Now look who's here!
The little madam herself!
Pretending once again she's been so awfully good!
Better not let me catch you slacking.
Better not catch my eye!
Ten rotten francs your mother sends me –
What is that going to buy?
Now, take that pail
My little 'Mademoiselle',
And go and draw some water from the well.
We should never have taken you in, in the first place.
How stupid the things that we do!
Like mother, like daughter, the scum of the street.
Eponine, come, my dear Eponine, let me see you:
You look very well in that new little blue little hat
There's *some* little girls who know how to behave
And they know what to wear
And I'm saying thank heaven for that.
Still there, Cosette?
Your tears will do you no good!
I told you fetch some water from the well in the
 wood . . .

COSETTE Please do not send me out alone,
Not in the darkness on my own!

MME THENARDIER Enough of that, or I'll forget to
 be nice!
You heard me ask for something
And I never ask twice!

*(The tavern fills up for the evening.)*

DRINKER 3 Come on, you old pest

DRINKER 2 Fetch a bottle of your best.

DRINKER 1 What's the nectar of the day?

THENARDIER Here, try this lot
Guaranteed to hit the spot
Or I'm not Thénardier

OTHER DRINKERS
4 Gissa glass of rum!
 Landlord, over here!

THENARDIER *(to himself)* Right away, you scum
*(to* CUSTOMER*)* Right away, M'sieur

DINERS
1 God, this place has gone to hell
2 So you tell me every year.

DRINKERS
6 Mine host Thénardier
 He was there, so they say,
 At the field of Waterloo.
7 Got there, it's true
 When the fight was all through,
1 But he knew just what to do.
 Crawling through the mud,
 So I've heard it said,
 Picking through the pockets
 of the English dead.
8 He made a tidy score
 From the spoils of war.

THENARDIER My band of soaks,
My den of dissolutes,
My dirty jokes, my always pissed as newts.
My sons of whores

Spend their lives in my inn,
Homing pigeons homing in.
They fly through my doors,
And their money's as good as yours.

EATER 1 Ain't got a clue
What he put into this stew –
Must've scraped it off the street.

EATER 2 God, what a wine!
Chateau Neuf de Turpentine –
Must've pressed it with his feet.

OTHER DRINKERS Landlord, over here!
Where's the bloody man?
One more for the road?
Thénardier, one more slug o' gin.
Just one more, or my old man is gonna do me in.

THENARDIER Welcome, M'sieur,
Sit yourself down,
And meet the best
Innkeeper in town.
As for the rest,
All of them crooks,
Rooking the guest
And cooking the books.
Seldom do you see
Honest men like me –
A gent of good intent
Who's content to be . . .

Master of the house,
Doling out the charm,
Ready with a handshake
And an open palm.
Tells a saucy tale,
Makes a little stir,
Customers appreciate a bon-viveur.
Glad to do a friend a favour –
Doesn't cost me to be nice.
But nothing gets you nothing
Everything has got a little price!

Master of the house,
Keeper of the zoo,
Ready to relieve 'em
Of a sou, or two.
Watering the wine,
Making up the weight,
Pickin' up their knick-knacks
When they can't see straight.
Everybody loves a landlord,
Everybody's bosom friend –
I do whatever pleases
Jesus! Won't I bleed 'em in the end!

THENARDIER & CHORUS Master of the house,
Quick to catch yer eye,
Never wants a passer-by
To pass him by.
Servant to the poor,
Butler to the great,
Comforter, philosopher
And lifelong mate!
Everybody's boon companion,
Everybody's chaperone . . .

THENARDIER But lock up your valises
Jesus! Won't I skin you to the bone!

Enter, M'sieur,
Lay down yer load,
Unlace yer boots
And rest from the road.
This weighs a ton,
Travel's a curse,
But here we strive
To lighten your purse.
Here the goose is cooked.
Here the fat is fried.
And nothing's overlooked
Till I'm satisfied . . .

Food beyond compare,
Food beyond belief,
Mix it in a mincer
And pretend it's beef.
Kidney of a horse,
Liver of a cat,
Filling up the sausages
With this and that!

Residents are more than welcome –
Bridal suite is occupied!
Reasonable charges
Plus some little extras on the side!

Charge 'em for the lice,
Extra for the mice,
Two per cent for looking in the mirror
  twice.
Here a little slice,
There a little cut,
Three per cent for sleeping with the window
  shut.
When it comes to fixing prices
There are lots of tricks he knows –
How it all increases,
All those bits and pieces
Jesus! It's amazing how it grows!

THENARDIER & CHORUS Master of the house,
Quick to catch your eye,
Never wants a passer-by to pass him by.
Servant to the poor,
Butler to the great,
Comforter, philosopher
And life-long mate.
Everybody's boon companion,
Gives 'em everything he's got . . .

THENARDIER Dirty bunch of geezers,
Jesus! What a sorry little lot!

MADAME THENARDIER I used to dream
That I would meet a prince.
But God Almighty,
Have you seen what's happened since?
'Master of the house'?
Isn't worth me spit!
'Comforter, philosopher!'
. . . and lifelong shit!
Cunning little brain,
Regular Voltaire.
Thinks he's quite a lover

But there's not much there.
What a cruel trick of nature,
Landed me with such a louse.
God knows how I've lasted
Living with this bastard in the house!

THENARDIER & CHORUS Master of the house

MADAME THENARDIER Master and a half!

THENARDIER & CHORUS Comforter, philosopher –

MADAME THENARDIER Don't make me laugh!

THENARDIER & CHORUS Servant to the poor,
Butler to the great –

MADAME THENARDIER Hypocrite and toady
And inebriate!

THENARDIER & CHORUS Everybody bless the
  landlord!
Everybody bless his spouse!

THENARDIER Everybody raise a glass.

MADAME THENARDIER Raise it up the master's arse.

ALL Everybody raise a glass ter the
  master of the house.

VALJEAN I found her wandering in the wood
This little child, I found her trembling in the shadows.
And I am here to help Cosette,
And I will settle any debt you may think proper.
I will pay what I must pay
To take Cosette away.
There is a duty I must heed,
There is a promise I have made.
For I was blind to one in need.
I did not see what stood before me,
Now her mother is with God –
Fantine's suffering is over
And I speak here with her voice,
And I stand here in her place.
And from this day and evermore.

MADAME THENARDIER Let me have your coat,
  M'sieur.

VALJEAN Cosette shall live in my protection.

THENARDIER You are very welcome here.

VALJEAN I will not forsake my vow.

THENARDIER Take a glass.

MADAME THENARDIER Take a chair.

VALJEAN Cosette shall have a father now!

THENARDIER What to do? What to say?
Shall you carry our treasure away?
What a gem! What a pearl!
Beyond rubies is our little girl!
How can we speak of debt?
Let's not haggle for darling Cosette!
Dear Fantine, gone to rest . . .
Have we done for her child what is best?
Shared our bread. Shared our bone.
Treated her like she's one of our own!
Like our own, Monsieur!

VALJEAN Your feelings do you credit, sir
And I will ease the parting blow.
Let us not talk of bargains or bones or greed
Now, may I say, we are agreed?

MADAME THENARDIER That would quite fit the bill
If she hadn't so often been ill.
Little dear, cost us dear,
Medicines are expensive, M'sieur!
Not that we begrudged a sou –
It's no more than we Christians must do!

THENARDIER & WIFE One thing more. One small
  doubt.
There are treacherous people about.
No offence. Please reflect.
Your intentions may not be correct?

VALJEAN No more words. Here's your price.
Fifteen hundred for your sacrifice.
Come, Cosette, say goodbye.
Let us seek out some friendlier sky.
Thank you both for Cosette.
It won't take you too long to forget.

Come, Cosette, come, my dear
From now on I will always be here
Where I go, you will be.

COSETTE Will there be children?
And castles to see?

VALJEAN Yes, Cosette,
Yes, it's true –
There's a castle just waiting for you.

VALJEAN & COSETTE La la la la la . . .

## 7. The Streets of Paris – Ten Years Later

BEGGARS' CHORUS Look down and see the beggars
  at your feet.
Look down and show some mercy if you can.
Look down and see
The sweepings of the street.
Look down, look down
Upon your fellow man!

GAVROCHE 'Ow do you do? My name's Gavroche.
These are my people. Here's my patch.
Not much to look at, nothing posh –
Nothing that you'd call up to scratch.
This is my school, my high society
Here in the slums of Saint Michel.
We live on crumbs of humble piety –
Tough on the teeth, but what the hell!
Think you're poor,
Think you're free,
Follow me! Follow me!

BEGGARS' CHORUS Look down and show some
  mercy if you can.
Look down, look down upon your fellow man.

OLD BEGGAR WOMAN What 'yer think yer at
Hanging round me pitch?
If you're new around here girl,
You've got a lot to learn.

YOUNG PROSTITUTE Listen, you old bat . . .
Crazy bloody witch . . .
'Least I give me customers
Some pleasure in return!

OLD BEGGAR WOMAN I know what you give.
Give 'em all the pox!
Spread around yer poison
Till they end up in a box.

PIMP Leave the poor old cow.
Move it, Madeleine.
She used to be no better
Till the clap got to her brain.

BEGGARS When's it gonna end?
When we gonna live?
Something's gotta happen now or
Something's gonna give
It'll come, it'll come, it'll come,
It'll come, it'll come, it'll come.

ENJOLRAS Where are the leaders of the land?
Where are the swells who run the show?

MARIUS Only one man – and that's Lamarque
Speaks for these people here below.

GAVROCHE Watch out for old Thénardier –
All of his family's on the make.
Once ran a hash-house down the way,
Bit of a swine and no mistake.
He's got a gang,
The bleeding layabout.
Even his daughter does her share –
That's Eponine, she knows her way about –
Only a kid but hard to scare.
Do we care?
Not a cuss!

Long live us.
Long live us!

BEGGARS Look down and show some mercy if you
  can.
Look down, look down
Upon your fellow man.

THENARDIER Everyone here, you know your place –
Brujon, Babet, Claquesous.
You, Montparnasse, watch for the law.
With Eponine take care
You turn on the tears,
No mistakes, my dears.

MADAME THENARDIER These bloody students on
  our streets.
Here they come slumming once again.
Our Eponine would kiss their feet,
She never had a scrap of brains.

MARIUS Hey, Eponine, what's up today?
I haven't seen you much about.

EPONINE Here, *you* always catch me in.

MARIUS Mind the police don't catch you *out*!

EPONINE 'Ere, wotcher do with all them books?
I coulda been a student, too!
Don't judge a girl on how she looks.
I know a *lot* of things, I do!

MARIUS Poor Eponine, the things you know
You wouldn't find in books like these.

EPONINE I like the way you grow your hair.

MARIUS I like the way you always tease.

EPONINE (*aside*) Little he knows!
Little he sees!

MADAME THENARDIER Here's the old boy. Stay on
  the job and watch out for the law.

EPONINE Stay out of this.

MARIUS But Eponine . . .

EPONINE You'll be in trouble here.
It's not your concern.
You'll be in the clear.

MARIUS Who is that man?

EPONINE Leave me alone!

MARIUS Why is he here? Hey, Eponine!
I didn't see you there, forgive me.

THENARDIER Please, m'sieur, come this way,
Here's a child that ain't eaten today.
Save a life, spare a sou –
God rewards all the good that you do.
Wait a bit. Know that face.
Ain't the world a remarkable place?
Men like me don't forget –
You're the bastard who borrowed Cosette!

VALJEAN What is this? Are you mad?
No, Monsieur, you don't know what you do!

THENARDIER You know me! You know me!
I'm a con, just like you.

EPONINE It's the police! Disappear!
Run for it! It's Javert!

JAVERT Another brawl in the square!
Another stink in the air!
Was there a witness to this?
Well, let him speak to Javert!
(*to* VALJEAN)
M'sieur, the streets are not safe,
but let these vermin beware.
We'll see that justice is done!

Look upon this fine collection
Crawled from underneath a stone
This swarm of worms and maggots
Could have picked you to the bone!
I know this man over here,
I know his name and his trade.
And on your witness, M'sieur,
We'll see him suitably paid.

(*He turns round to find* VALJEAN *gone*)

JAVERT But where's the gentleman gone?
And why on earth did he run?

THENARDIER You will have a job to catch him.
*He's* the one you should arrest!
No more bourgeois when you scratch him
Than that brand upon his chest!

JAVERT Could it be he's some old gaolbird
That the tide now washes in?
Heard my name and started running
Had the brand upon his skin!
And the girl who stood beside him
When I turned they both had gone.
Could he be the man I hunted?
Could it be he's Jean Valjean?

THENARDIER In the absence of a victim
Dear Inspector, may I go?
And remember when you've nicked 'im
It was me that told you so!

JAVERT (*aside*) Let the old man keep on running.
I will run him off his feet!
(*to the crowd*)
Everyone about your business!

Clear this garbage
Off the street!

There, out in the darkness,
A fugitive running,
Fallen from grace.
Fallen from grace.
God be my witness,
I never shall yield
Till we come face to face.
Till we come face to face.

He knows his way in the dark.
Mine is the way of the Lord.
Those who do follow the path of the righteous
Shall have their reward,
And if they fall
As Lucifer fell,
The flame,
The sword.

Stars in your multitudes,
Scarce to be counted,
Filling the darkness
With order and light.
You are the sentinels,
Silent and sure.
Keeping watch in the night
Keeping watch in the night.

You know your place in the sky,
You hold your course
And your aim,
And each in your season
Returns and returns
And is always the same.
And if you fall
As Lucifer fell
You fall
In flame.

And so it has been and so it's written
On the doorway to paradise
That those who falter
And those who fall
Must pay
The price.

Lord let me find him,
That I may see him
Safe behind bars.
I will never rest
Till then.
This I swear,
This I swear by the stars.

GAVROCHE That inspector thinks he's something
But it's me who runs this town!
And my theatre never closes
And the curtain's never down.

Trust Gavroche. Have no fear.
Don't you worry, Auntie dear,
You can always find me here.

EPONINE Cosette! Now I remember
Cosette! How can it be
We were children together
Look what's become of me . . .

Good God! Ooh, what a rumpus!

MARIUS That girl! Who can she be?

EPONINE That cop! He'd like to jump us
But he ain't smart, not he.

MARIUS Eponine, who was that girl?

EPONINE That bourgeois two-a-penny thing!

MARIUS Eponine, find her for me!

EPONINE What will you give me?

MARIUS Anything!

EPONINE Got you all excited now
But God knows what you see in her.
Ain't you all delighted now?

No, I don't want your money, sir . . .

MARIUS Eponine! Do this for me . . .
Discover where she lives,
Be careful how you go.
Don't let your father know
'Ponine! I'm lost until she's found!

EPONINE Y'see! I told you so!
There's lots of things I know
'Ponine . . . she knows her way around.

## 8. Café of the ABC Friends

COMBEFERRE At Notre Dame
The sections are prepared!

FEUILLY At rue du Bac
They're straining at the leash!

COURFEYRAC Students, workers, everyone.
There's a river on the run:
Like the flowing of the tide
Paris coming to our side!

ENJOLRAS The time is near,
So near it's stirring the blood in their veins.
And yet beware,
Don't let the wine go to your brains,
For the army we fight is a dangerous foe,
With the men and the arms that we never can match.
It is easy to sit here and swat 'em like flies
But the National Guard will be harder to catch.
We need a sign
To rally the people,
To call them to arms,
To bring them in line.
Marius, you're late.

JOLY What's wrong today?
You look as if you've seen a ghost.

GRANTAIRE Some wine, and say what's going on.

MARIUS A ghost you say, a ghost maybe . . .
She was just like a ghost to me
One minute there . . . then she was gone!

GRANTAIRE I am agog!
I am aghast!
Is Marius in love at last?
I have never seen him 'ooh' and 'aah'.
You talk of battles to be won
And here he comes like Don Ju-an –
It's better than an o-per-a!

ENJOLRAS It is time for us all
To decide who we are.
Do we fight for the right
To a night at the opera now?
Have you asked of yourselves
What's the price you might pay?
Is it simply a game
For rich young boys to play?
The colour of the world
Is changing day by day . . .
Red – the blood of angry men!
Black – the dark of ages past
Red – a world about to dawn!
Black – the night that ends at last!

MARIUS Had you been there tonight,
You might know how it feels
To be struck to the bone
In a moment of breathless delight!
Had you been there tonight
You might also have known
How the world may be changed
In just one burst of light.
And what was right seems wrong
And what was wrong seems right!
Red – I feel my soul on fire!
Black – my world if she's not there!
Red – the colour of desire!
Black – the colour of despair!

ENJOLRAS Marius, you're no longer a child.
I do not doubt you mean it well
But now there is a higher call.
Who cares about your lonely soul?
We strive towards a larger goal –
Our little lives don't count at all!

STUDENTS Red – the blood of angry men!
Black – the dark of ages past!
Red – a world about to dawn!
Black – the night that ends at last!

ENJOLRAS Well, Courfeyrac, do we have all the guns?
Feuilly, Combeferre, our time is running short.
Grantaire, put the bottle down!
Do we have the guns we need?

GRANTAIRE Give me brandy on my breath.
And I'll breathe them all to death!

COURFEYRAC In St Antoine they're with us to a man!

COMBEFERRE In Notre Dame they're tearing up the
stones.

FEUILLY Twenty rifles good as new!

GAVROCHE Listen!

JOLY Twenty rounds for every man!

GAVROCHE Listen to me!

PROUVAIRE Double that in Port St Cloud!

GAVROCHE Listen, everybody!

LESGLES Seven guns in St Martin!

GAVROCHE General Lamarque is dead!

ENJOLRAS Lamarque is dead.
Lamarque. His death is the hour of fate.
The people's man.
His death is the sign we await.
On his funeral day they will honour his name.
It's a rallying cry that will reach every ear!
In the death of Lamarque we will kindle the flame –
They will see that the day of salvation is near.
The time is here!
Let us welcome it gladly with courage and cheer,
Let us take to the streets with no doubt in our hearts.
But a jubilant shout
They will come one and all,
They will come when we call!

ENJOLRAS Do you hear the people sing?
Singing the song of angry men?
It is the music of a people
Who will not be slaves again!
When the beating of your heart
Echoes the beating of the drums,
There is a life about to start
When tomorrow comes!

COMBEFERRE Will you join in our crusade?
Who will be strong and stand with me?
Beyond the barricade
Is there a world you long to see?

COURFEYRAC Then join in the fight
That will give you the right to be free.

CHORUS Do you hear the people sing?
Singing the song of angry men?
It is the music of a people
Who will not be slaves again!
When the beating of your heart
Echoes the beating of the drums,
There is a life about to start
When tomorrow comes!

FEUILLY Will you give all you can give
So that our banner may advance?
Some will fall and some will live –
Will you come up and take your chance?
The blood of the martyrs
Will water the meadows of France!

CHORUS Do you hear the people sing?
Singing the song of angry men?
It is the music of a people
Who will not be slaves again!
When the beating of your heart
Echoes the beating of the drums,
There is a life about to start
When tomorrow comes!

## 9. The Rue Plumet

COSETTE How strange this feeling that my life's begun
at last.
This change, can people really fall in love so fast?
What's the matter with you, Cosette?

Have you been too much on your own?
So many things unclear,
So many things unknown.

In my life
There are so many questions and answers
That somehow seem wrong.
In my life
There are times when I catch in the silence
The sigh of a faraway song.
And it sings
Of a world that I long to see,
Out of reach,
Just a whisper away . . .
Waiting for me.

Does he know I'm alive?
Do I know if he's real?
Does he see what I saw?
Does he feel what I feel?

In my life
I'm no longer alone
Now the love in my life
Is so near.
Find me now, find me here.

VALJEAN Dear Cosette,
You're such a lonely child.
How pensive, how sad you seem to me.
Believe me, were it within my power
I'd fill each passing hour.
How quiet it must be, I can see,
With only me for company.

COSETTE There's so little I know
That I'm longing to know
Of the child that I was
In a time long ago . . .
There's so little you say
Of the life you have known,
Why you keep to yourself
Why we're always alone.
So dark! So dark and deep . . .
The secrets that you keep!

In my life
I have all that I want –
You are loving and gentle and good.
But Papa, dear Papa,
In your eyes I am lost like a child
Who is lost in a wood.

VALJEAN No more words,
No more words. It's a time that is dead.
There are words
That are better unheard,
Better unsaid.

COSETTE In my life
I'm no longer a child and I yearn
For the truth that you know
Of the years . . . years ago!

VALJEAN You will learn
Truth is given by God
To us all in our time,
In our turn.

MARIUS In my life
She has burst like the music of angels

The light of the sun!
And my life seems to stop
As if something is over
And something has scarcely begun.
Eponine, you're the friend
Who has brought me here.
Thanks to you, I am one with the gods
And heaven is near!
And I soar through a world that is new, that is free.

EPONINE (aside)
Every word that he says
Is a dagger in me!
In my life
There's been no one like him anywhere,
Anywhere, where he is
If he asked . . . I'd be his!

MARIUS & EPONINE In my life, there is someone
  who touches my life,

MARIUS Waiting near!

EPONINE Waiting here!

MARIUS A heart full of love,
A heart full of song,
I'm doing everything all wrong.
Oh God, for shame
I do not even know your name,
Dear Mad'moiselle.
Won't you say,
Will you tell?

COSETTE A heart full of love –
No fear, no regret.

MARIUS My name is Marius Pontmercy.

COSETTE And mine's Cosette.

MARIUS Cosette, I don't know what to say.

COSETTE Then make no sound.

MARIUS I am lost . . .

COSETTE I am found.

MARIUS A heart full of light,

COSETTE A night bright as day.

MARIUS And you must never go away
Cosette, Cosette!

COSETTE This is a chain we'll never break.

MARIUS Do I dream?

COSETTE I'm awake.

| MARIUS | EPONINE |
|---|---|
| A heart full of love | He was never mine to lose. |
| | Why regret |
| COSETTE | What could not be? |
| A heart full of you | |
| | Those are words |
| MARIUS | He'll never say, |
| A single look and then I | Not to me. |
| knew | |
| | Not to me, |
| COSETTE | Not to me. |
| I knew it too. | |
| | His heart |
| MARIUS | |
| From today | Full of love, |
| | He will never |
| COSETTE | Feel this way. |
| Every day | |

COSETTE & MARIUS For it isn't a dream,
Not a dream
After all.

EPONINE 'Parnasse, what are you doing
So far out of our patch?

MONTPARNASSE This house, we're going to do it.
Rich man, plenty of scratch –
You remember he's the one
Who got away the other day.
Got a number on his chest,
Perhaps a fortune put away!

EPONINE O Lord, somebody help me!
Dear God, what'll I do?
He'll think
This is an ambush.
He'll think I'm in it, too!

What'll I do? What'll I say?
I've got to warn them here.
I gotta find a way!

## 10. The Attempted Robbery

THENARDIER This is his lair:
I've seen the old fox around,
He keeps himself to himself,
He's staying close to the ground.
I smell profit here.

Ten years ago
He came and paid for Cosette.
I let her go for a song –

It's time we settled the debt.
This'll cost him dear.

BRUJON What do I care
Who you should rob?
Gimme my share
Finish the job!

THENARDIER You shut your mouth,
Give me your hand.

BRUJON What have we here?

THENARDIER Who is this hussy?

BABET It's your brat Eponine –
Don't you know your own kid?
Why's she hanging about you?

THENARDIER Eponine, get on home;
You're not needed in this,
We're enough here without you.

EPONINE I know this house
I tell you there's nothing here for you.
Just the old man and the girl,
They live ordinary lives.

THENARDIER Don't interfere
You've got some gall
Take care, young miss
You've got a lot to say!

BRUJON She's going soft.

CLAQUESOUS Happens to all.

MONTPARNASSE Go home, 'Ponine
Go home, you're in the way.

EPONINE I'm gonna scream, I'm gonna warn them here.

THENARDIER One little scream and you'll regret it
For a year.

CLAQUESOUS What a palaver
What an absolute treat
To watch a cat and its father
Pick a bone in the street.

BRUJON Not a sound out of you!

EPONINE Well, I told you I'd do it
Told you I'd do it . . .

(*She screams*)

THENARDIER (*breaking it up*) You wait my girl, you'll
rue this night.
I'll make you scream. You'll scream alright.
Leave her to me. Don't wait around.
Make for the sewers. Go underground.

MARIUS It was your cry sent them away –
Once more, 'Ponine, saving the day!
Dearest Cosette – my friend 'Ponine
Brought me to you,
Showed me the way!

Someone is near.
Let's not be seen –
Somebody's here.

VALJEAN My God, Cosette!
I heard a cry in the dark,
I heard the shout of angry voices in the street.

COSETTE That was my cry you heard, Papa,
I was afraid of what they'd do.
They ran away when they heard my cry.

VALJEAN Cosette, my child, what will become of you?

COSETTE Three men I saw beyond the wall,
Three men in shadow moving fast!

VALJEAN This is a warning to us all,
These are the shadows of the past!
(*Aside*)
Must be Javert!
He's found my cover at last!
I've got to get Cosette away
Before they return!

We must get away from shadows
That will never let us be.
Tomorrow to Calais.
And then a ship across the sea!
Hurry, Cosette, prepare to leave and say no more,
Tomorrow we'll away!
Hurry, Cosette, it's time to close another door
And live another day!

## 11. *Act One Finale*

VALJEAN One day more!
Another day, another destiny.
This never-ending road to Calvary,
These men who seem to know my crime
Will surely come a second time.
One day more!

MARIUS I did not live until today.
How can I live when we are parted?

VALJEAN One day more.

MARIUS & COSETTE Tomorrow you'll be worlds
away
And yet with you my world has started!

EPONINE One more day all on my own.

MARIUS & COSETTE Will we ever meet again?

EPONINE One more day with him not caring.

MARIUS & COSETTE I was born to be with you.

EPONINE What a life I might have known.

MARIUS & COSETTE And I swear I will be true.

EPONINE But he never saw me there!

ENJOLRAS One more day before the storm!

MARIUS Do I follow where she goes?

ENJOLRAS At the barricades of freedom.

MARIUS Shall I join my brothers there?

ENJOLRAS When our ranks begin to form.

MARIUS Do I stay: and do I dare?

ENJOLRAS Will you take your place with me?

CHORUS The time is now,
The day is here.

VALJEAN One day more!

JAVERT One day more to revolution,
We will nip it in the bud.
We'll be ready for these schoolboys,
They will wet themselves . . . with blood!

VALJEAN One day more.

THENARDIER Watch 'em run amuck,
Catch 'em as they fall,
Never know your luck
When there's a free-for-all.
Here a little 'dip',
There a little 'touch',
Most of them are goners
So they won't miss much!

REBEL STUDENTS One day to a new beginning.
Raise the flag of freedom high.
Every man will be a king,
Every man will be a king.
There's a new world for the winning,
There's a new world to be won.

MARIUS My place is here,
I fight with you.

VALJEAN One day more.

| MARIUS & COSETTE | JAVERT | EPONINE |
|---|---|---|
| I did not live until today. | I will join these people's heroes | |
| | I will follow where they go. | One more day on my own. |
| How can I live when we are parted? | I will learn their little secrets, | |
| | I will know the things they know. | |

VALJEAN One day more.

| MARIUS & COSETTE | JAVERT | THENARDIER |
|---|---|---|
| Tomorrow you'll be worlds away. | One more day to revolution. | Watch 'em run amuck, Catch 'em as they fall, |
| | We will nip it in the bud. | Never know your luck When there's a free for all. |
| And yet with you my world has started. | We'll be ready for these schoolboys. | |

VALJEAN Tomorrow we'll be far away
Tomorrow is the judgment day. Tomorrow is the judgment day.

ALL Tomorrow we'll discover
What our God in Heaven has in store
One more dawn
One more day
One day more.

# ACT TWO

## 1. A Street in Paris

(ENJOLRAS *addresses all the students*)

ENJOLRAS Here upon these stones
We will build our barricade,
In the heart of the city
We claim as our own.
Each man to his duty
And don't be afraid.
Wait!
I will need a report
On the strength of the foe.

JAVERT (*disguised as a rebel*) I can find out the truth.
I know their ways,
Fought their wars,
Served my time,
In the days
Of my youth.

PROUVAIRE Now the people will fight.

GRANTAIRE And so they might.
Dogs will bark,
Fleas will bite.

LESGLES They will do what is right!

MARIUS Hey, little boy, who's this I see?
God, Eponine, the things you do!

EPONINE I know this is no place for me
Still I would rather be with you!

MARIUS Get out before the trouble starts.
Get out, 'Ponine, you might get shot!

EPONINE I got you worried now, I have,
That shows you like me quite a lot!

MARIUS There is a way that you can help,
You are the answer to a prayer!
Please take this letter to Cosette
And pray to God that she's still there!

EPONINE Little you know!
Little you care!

## 2. The Rue Plumet

EPONINE I have a letter, M'sieur;
It's addressed to your daughter, Cosette.
It's from a boy at the barricade, sir,
In the rue de Villette.

VALJEAN Give me that letter here, my boy.

EPONINE He said to give it to Cosette!

VALJEAN You have my word that my daughter will know
What this letter contains.
Tell the young man she will read it tomorrow.

And here's for your pains.
Go careful now. Stay out of sight.
There's danger in the streets tonight!

(*opens and reads the letter*)

'Dearest Cosette, you have entered my soul
And soon you will be gone.
Can it be only a day since we met
And the world was reborn?
If I should fall in the battle to come
Let this be my Goodbye . . .
Now that I know that you love me as well
It is harder to die . . .
I pray that God will bring me home
To be with you.
Pray for your Marius. He prays for you!'

EPONINE And now I'm all alone again,
Nowhere to turn, no-one to go to,
Without a home, without a friend,
Without a face to say hello to.

And now the night is near, now I can make
Believe he's here.

Sometimes I walk alone at night
When everybody else is sleeping.
I think of him and then I'm happy
With the company I'm keeping.
The city goes to bed
And I can live inside my head.

On my own,
Pretending he's beside me.
All alone, I walk with him till morning.
Without him
I feel his arms around me,
And when I lose my way I close my eyes
And he has found me.

In the rain the pavement shines like silver,
All the lights are misty in the river.
In the darkness the trees are full of starlight,
And all I see is him and me for ever and forever.

And I know it's only in my mind,
That I'm talking to myself and not to him.

And although I know that he is blind,
Still I say there's a way for us.

I love him
But when the night is over,
He is gone, the river's just a river.
Without him the world around me changes,
The trees are bare and everywhere the streets
Are full of strangers.

I love him
But everyday I'm learning.
All my life I've only been pretending.
Without me his world will go on turning,
A world that's full of happiness that I have never
  known.
I love him, I love him,
I love him, but only on my own.

## 3. At the Barricade

COMBEFERRE, FEUILLY, COURFEYRAC,
  PROUVAIRE Now we pledge ourselves to hold this
barricade.

MARIUS Let them come in their legions
And they will be met!

ENJOLRAS Have faith in yourselves
And don't be afraid.

GRANTAIRE Let's give 'em a screwing
They'll never forget.

COMBEFERRE This is where it begins.

COURFEYRAC And if I should die in the fight to be
  free,

Where the fighting is hardest –
There will I be.

FEUILLY Let them come if they dare
We'll be there!

ARMY OFFICER You at the barricade, listen to this!
No one is coming to help you to fight!
You're on your own,
You have no friends
Give up your guns – or die!

ENJOLRAS Damn their warnings. Damn their lies!
They will see the people rise!

ENJOLRAS & ALL Damn their warnings. Damn their
  lies!
They will see the people rise!

SENTRY (JOLY) He's back.

JAVERT Listen, my friends,
I have done as I said.
I have been to their lines,
I have counted each man.
I will tell what I can:
Better be warned.
They have armies to spare
And our danger is real.
We will need all our cunning
To bring them to heel.

ENJOLRAS Have faith!
If you know what their movements are
We'll spoil their game.
There are ways that a people can fight –
We shall overcome their power.

JAVERT I have overheard their plans
There will be no attack tonight.
They intend to starve you out
Before they start a proper fight.
Concentrate their force
Hit us from the right.

GAVROCHE Liar.
Good evening, dear Inspector
Lovely evening, my dear.
I know this man, my friends
His name's Inspector Javert.
So don't believe a word he says
'Cause none of it's true.
This only goes to show
What little people can do.

And little people know
When little people fight.
We may look easy pickings
But we got some bite.
So never kick a dog
Because he's just a pup.
We'll fight like twenty armies
And we won't give up!
So you'd better run for cover
When the pup grows up.

GRANTAIRE Bravo, little Gavroche! You're the top of
  the class!

PROUVAIRE So what are we going to do
With this snake in the grass?

ENJOLRAS Tie this man and take him
To the tavern in there.
The people will decide your fate,
Inspector Javert!

COURFEYRAC Take the bastard now and shoot him!

FEUILLY Let us watch the devil dance!

LESGLES You'd have done the same, Inspector
If we'd let you have your chance!

JAVERT Shoot me now or shoot me later
Every schoolboy to his sport!
Death to each and every traitor!
I renounce your people's court.

COMBEFERRE Though we may not all survive here
There are things that never die.

GRANTAIRE What's the difference, die a schoolboy
Die a policeman, die a spy.

ENJOLRAS Take this man. Bring him through.
There is work we have to do.

JOLY There's a boy climbing the barricade.

MARIUS Good God! What are you doing?
'Ponine! Have you no fear?
Have you seen my beloved?
Why have you come back here?

EPONINE Took your letter like you said.
I met her father at the door.
He said he would give it
(EPONINE *falls*)
I don't think I can stand any more.

MARIUS Eponine, what's wrong? I feel
There's something wet upon your hair . . .

Eponine, you're hurt!
You need some help. Oh God,
It's everywhere!

EPONINE Don't you fret, M'sieur Marius,
I don't feel any pain,
A little fall of rain
Can hardly hurt me now.
You're here. That's all I need to know.
And you will keep me safe,
And you will keep me close,
And rain will make the flowers grow.

MARIUS But you will live, 'Ponine – dear God above,
If I could heal your wounds with words of love.

EPONINE Just hold me now, and let it be.
Shelter me, comfort me.

MARIUS You would live a hundred years
If I could show you how
I won't desert you now . . .

EPONINE The rain can't hurt me now.
This rain will wash away what's past
And you will keep me safe,
And you will keep me close.
I'll sleep in your embrace at last.

EPONINE
The rain that brings you
  here
Is heaven blessed.
The skies begin to clear

MARIUS

And I'm at rest.
A breath away from where
  you are,
I've come home from so
  far.
So don't you fret, M'sieur
  Marius,
I don't feel any pain.
A little fall of rain
Can hardly hurt me now.
That's all I need to know.
And you will keep me safe,
And you will keep me close,
And rain
Will make the flowers . . .

Hush-a-bye, dear Eponine,
You won't feel any pain.
A little fall of rain
Can hardly hurt you now.
I'm here.
I will stay with you till you
  are sleeping.
And rain
Will make the flowers

Grow.

(EPONINE *dies*)

ENJOLRAS She is the first to fall.
The first of us to fall upon this barricade.

MARIUS Her name was Eponine.
Her life was cold and dark yet she was unafraid.

COMBEFERRE We fight here in her name.

PROUVAIRE She will not die in vain.

LESGLES She will not be betrayed.

JOLY Here comes a man in uniform
What brings you to this place?

VALJEAN I come here as a volunteer.

JOLY Approach and show your face.

SENTRY You wear an army uniform.

VALJEAN That's why they let me through.

JOLY You've got some years behind you, sir.

VALJEAN There's much that I can do.

JOLY You see that prisoner over there?

GRANTAIRE A volunteer like you!

COMBEFERRE A spy! who calls himself Javert!

GRANTAIRE He's going to get it, too!

SENTRY They're getting ready to attack.

(ENJOLRAS *gives the unarmed* VALJEAN *a gun*)

ENJOLRAS Take this and use it well!
But if you shoot us in the back
You'll never live to tell.

STUDENT 1 Platoon of sappers advancing towards the
  barricade.

STUDENT 2 Troops behind them! Fifty men or more!

(*A fierce attack is launched on the barricade*)

ENJOLRAS Fire!

(*The Attack*)

FEUILLY Sniper!

LESGLES See how they run away!

GRANTAIRE By God, we've won the day!

ENJOLRAS They will be back again.
Make an attack again.

For your presence of mind,
For the deed you have done,
I will thank you, M'sieur
When our battle is won.

VALJEAN Give me no thanks, M'sieur
There's something you can do.

ENJOLRAS If it is in my power.

VALJEAN Give me the spy Javert –
Let me take care of him!

JAVERT The law is inside out,
The world is upside down.

ENJOLRAS Do what you have to do,
The man belongs to you.

The enemy may be regrouping. Hold yourself in
  readiness. Come, my friends, back to your positions,
  the night is falling fast.

VALJEAN We meet again.

JAVERT You've hungered for this all your life;
Take your revenge!
How right you should kill with a knife!

(VALJEAN *cuts* JAVERT's *bonds*)

VALJEAN You talk too much,
Your life is safe in my hands.

JAVERT Don't understand.

VALJEAN Get out of here.

JAVERT Valjean, take care!
I'm warning you . . .

VALJEAN Clear out of here.

JAVERT Once a thief, forever a thief.
What you want you always steal!
You would trade your life for mine.
Yes, Valjean, you want a deal!
Shoot me now, for all I care!

If you let me go, beware,
You'll still answer to Javert!

VALJEAN You are wrong, and always have been wrong.
I'm a man no worse than any man.
You are free and there are no conditions,
No bargains or petitions.
There's nothing that I blame you for.
You've done your duty, nothing more.
If I come out of this alive you'll find me
At number fifty-five rue Plumet
No doubt our paths will cross again

(VALJEAN *fires a gun into the air.* JAVERT *goes*)

ENJOLRAS Courfeyrac, you take the watch.
They won't attack until it's light.
Everybody, stay awake,
We must be ready for the fight.
For the final fight
Let no one sleep tonight!
Marius, rest.

FEUILLY Drink with me to days gone by.
Sing with me the songs we knew.

PROUVAIRE Here's to pretty girls
Who went to our heads.

JOLY Here's to witty girls
Who went to our beds.

ALL THREE Here's to them
And here's to you!

GRANTAIRE Drink with me to days gone by.
Can it be you fear to die?
Will the world remember you
When you fall?
Can it be your death
Means nothing at all?
Is your life just one more lie?

| MEN | WOMEN |
|---|---|
| Drink with me | Drink with me |
| To days | To days |
| Gone by. | Gone by. |
| To the life | To the life |
| That used | That used |
| To be. | To be. |
| | At the shrine of friendship |
| | Never say die, |
| Let the wine of friendship | |
| Never run dry. Here's to | |
|   you | |
| And here's | Here's to you |
| To me. | And here's |
| | To me. |

MARIUS Do I care if I should die
Now she goes across the sea?
Life without Cosette
Means nothing at all.
Would you weep, Cosette,
Should Marius fall?
Will you weep,
Cosette,
For me?

VALJEAN God on high,
Hear my prayer –
In my need
You have always been there.
He is young,
He's afraid –
Let him rest,
Heavens blessed.
Bring him home,
Bring him home,
Bring him home.
He's like the son I might have known
If God had granted me a son.
The summers die
One by one.
How soon they fly
On and on.
And I am old
And will be gone.
Bring him peace,
Bring him joy.
He is young,
He is only a boy.
You can take,
You can give –
Let him be,
Let him live.
If I die, let me die –
Let him live, bring him home,
Bring him home,
Bring him home.

*(Dawn breaks)*

ENJOLRAS The people have not stirred.
We are abandoned by those
Who still live in fear.
The people have not heard.
Yet we will not abandon those
Who cannot hear.
Let us not waste lives.
Let all the women and fathers of children
Go from here.

FEUILLY Drink with me to days gone by.
Sing with me the songs we knew.

ALL At the shrine of friendship
Raise your glass high.
Let the wine of friendship
Never run dry.
If I die
I die with you!

ENJOLRAS How do we stand, Feuilly?
Make your report.

FEUILLY We've guns enough
But ammunition short.

MARIUS Let me go into the streets.
There are bodies all around,
Ammunition to be had,
Lots of bullets to be found!

ENJOLRAS I won't let you go –
It's too much of a chance.

MARIUS The same is true
For any man here!

VALJEAN Let me go!
He's no more than a boy.
I am old,
I have nothing to fear.

*(GAVROCHE is already climbing the barricade)*

GAVROCHE You need somebody quicker
And I volunteer!

LESGLES Come back, Gavroche, don't you dare!

JOLY Someone pull him down at once!

GAVROCHE Look at me, I'm almost there!
Little people know, when
Little people fight, we
May look easy pickings
But we've got some bite.
So never kick a dog
Because it's just a pup.
We'll fight like twenty armies
And we won't give up.
So you'd better run for cover
When the pup grows . . .

*(GAVROCHE dies)*

LOUDHAILER VOICE You at the barricade, listen to
  this:
The people of Paris sleep in their beds.
You have no chance,
No chance at all.
Why throw your lives away?

## 4. The Battle

ENJOLRAS Let us die facing our foes –
Make them bleed while we can.

COMBEFERRE Make 'em pay through the nose.

COURFEYRAC Make 'em pay for every man.

ENJOLRAS Let others rise
To take our place
Until the earth is free!

(*All on the barricade are killed, except for* VALJEAN *and* MARIUS *who is wounded and unconscious.*

VALJEAN *rescues him and carries him down a manhole into the sewers.*

*As they disappear,* JAVERT *returns to the barricade. He searches for* VALJEAN *among the bodies. Not finding him he realises* VALJEAN *has escaped by the only possible way – into the sewers*)

## 5. The Sewer – Dog Eats Dog

(THENARDIER *appears in the sewers with a body over his shoulders.*)

THENARDIER Here's a hint of gold
Stuck into a tooth –
Pardon me, M'sieur
You won't be using this no more:
Shouldn't be too hard to sell.
Add it to the pile,
Add it to the stock.
Here, among the sewer rats –
A breath away from Hell –
Y'get accustomed to the smell.

Well, someone's got to clean 'em up, my friends –
Bodies on the highway,
Law and order upside down.
Someone's got to collect their odds and ends
As a service to the town.

Here's a tasty ring,
Pretty little thing –
Wouldn't want to waste it
That would really be a crime.
Thank you, sir, I'm in your debt.
Here's another toy.
Take it off the boy –
His heart's no longer going
And he's lived his little time.

Well, someone's got to clean them up, my friends
Before the little harvest
Disappears into the mud.
Someone's got to collect their odds and ends
When the gutters run with blood.

It's a world where the dogs eat the dogs,
Where they kill for the bones in the street,
And God in his Heaven
He don't interfere
'Cos he's dead as the stiff at my feet.
I raise my eyes to see the heavens
And only the moon looks down,
The harvest moon shines down.

(THENARDIER *goes to rob* VALJEAN, *but suddenly recognises him and runs away.*

VALJEAN *recovers, picks up* MARIUS *and continues his journey through the sewers*)

(*Musical Sequence*)

VALJEAN It's you, Javert!
I knew you wouldn't wait too long –

The faithful servant at his post once more!
This man's done no wrong
And he needs a doctor's care.

JAVERT I warned you I would not give in,
I won't be swayed.

VALJEAN Another hour yet
And then I'm yours
And all our debts are paid.

JAVERT The man of mercy
Comes again
And talks of justice.

VALJEAN Come, time is running short.
Look down, Javert,
He's standing in his grave.
Give way, Javert,
There is a life to save.

JAVERT Take him, Valjean
Before I change my mind.
I will be waiting
24601.

## 6. A Bridge over the Seine

JAVERT Who is this man?
What sort of devil is he
To have me caught in a trap
And choose to let me go free?
It was his hour at last
To put a seal on my fate,
Wipe out the past
And wash me clean off the slate.
All it would take
Was a flick of his knife.
Vengeance was his and he gave me back my life!

Damned if I'll live in the debt of a thief.
Damned if I'll yield at the end of the chase.
I am the Law and the Law is not mocked,
I'll spit his pity right back in his face.
There is nothing on earth that we share,
It is either Valjean or Javert!

How can I now allow this man
To hold dominion over me?
This desperate man that I have hunted,
He gave me my life. He gave me freedom.

I should have perished by his hand,
It was his right.
It was my right to die as well.
Instead, I live . . . but live in hell.

And my thoughts fly apart,
Can this man be believed?
Shall his sins be forgiven?
Shall his crimes be reprieved?

And must I now begin to doubt,
Who never doubted all those years?
My heart is stone and still it trembles.
The world I have known is lost in shadow.
Is he from heaven or from hell?
And does he know
That, granting me my life today
This man has killed me even so?

I am reaching but I fall
And the stars are black and cold,
As I stare into the void
Of a world that cannot hold.
I'll escape now from the world,
From the world of Jean Valjean.
There is nowhere I can go.
There is no way to go on . . .

*(He throws himself into the swollen river)*

WOMEN Did you see them
Going off to fight?
Children of the barricade
Who didn't last the night?
Did you see them
Lying where they died?
Someone used to cradle them
And kiss them when they cried.
Did you see them lying side by side?
Who will wake them?
No one ever will.
No one ever told them
That a summer day can kill.
They were schoolboys.
Never held a gun . . .
Fighting for a new world
That would rise up with the sun.
Where's that new world now the fighting's done?

Nothing changes. Nothing ever will.
Every year another brat, another mouth to fill.
Same old story. What's the use of tears?
What's the use of praying
If there's nobody who hears?
Turning, turning, turning, turning, turning
Through the years.

Turning, turning, turning through the years.
Minutes into hours, and the hours into years.
Nothing changes. Nothing ever can.
Round about the roundabout, and back where you
  began.

ALL Round and round and back where you began!

MARIUS There's a grief that can't be spoken.
There's a pain goes on and on.
Empty chairs at empty tables
Now my friends are dead and gone.

Here they talked of revolution.
Here it was they lit the flame.
Here they sang about 'tomorrow'
And tomorrow never came.

From the table in the corner
They could see a world reborn,
And they rose with voices ringing
I can hear them now.
The very words that they had sung
Became their last communion
On the lonely barricade at dawn.

Oh my friends, my friends, forgive me
That I live and you are gone.
There's a grief that can't be spoken.
There's a pain goes on and on.

Phantom faces at the window.
Phantom shadows on the floor.
Empty chairs at empty tables
Where my friends will meet no more.

Oh my friends, my friends, don't ask me
What your sacrifice was for.
Empty chairs at empty tables
Where my friends will sing no more.

*(Time has passed. Suggest* MARIUS *convalescing,
  encouraged by* COSETTE *who takes his arm as he walks
  with firmer step)*

COSETTE Every day
You walk with stronger step,
You walk with longer step –
'The worst is over'.

MARIUS Every day
I wonder, every day,
Who it was brought me here
From the barricade?

COSETTE Don't think about it, Marius!
With all the years ahead of us!
I will never go away
And we will be together
'Every day',
Every day.
We'll remember that night
And the song that we sang –
A heart full of love.

A night full of you.

The words are old
But always true.
Oh, God for shame
You did not even know my name!

MARIUS Dear Mad'moiselle
I was lost in your spell.

COSETTE
A heart full of love.

No fear nor regret.
'My name is Marius
  Pontmercy.'

MARIUS Cosette, Cosette.

COSETTE
I saw you waiting and I
  knew.

MARIUS
Waiting for you
At your feet.

COSETTE
At your call.

MARIUS & COSETTE
And it wasn't a dream,
Not a dream after all.

VALJEAN
She was never mine to
  keep.

She is youthful, she is free.

VALJEAN
Love is the garden of the
  young.

Let it be.

Let it be.

A heart full of love,
This I give you this day.

MARIUS M'sieur, this is a day
I never can forget.
Is gratitude enough
For giving me Cosette?
Your home shall be with us
And not a day shall pass.
But we will prove our love
To you, whom we shall call
A father to us both,
A father to us all.

VALJEAN Not another word, my son
There's something now that must be done.
You've spoken from the heart
And I must do the same.
There is a story, sir,
Of slavery and shame
That you alone must know.

I never told Cosette
She had enough of tears.
She's never known the truth –
The story you must hear
Of years ago.

There lived a man whose name was Jean Valjean,
He stole some bread to save his sister's son.
For nineteen winters served his time
In sweat he washed away his crime.
Years ago
He broke parole and lived a life apart.
How could he tell Cosette and break her heart?
It's for Cosette this must be faced –
If he is caught she is disgraced.
The time has come to journey on
And from this day he must be gone
Who am I?
Who am I?

MARIUS You're Jean Valjean!
What can I do
That will turn you from this?
Monsieur, you cannot leave.
Whatever I tell my beloved Cosette
She will never believe!

VALJEAN Make her believe
I have gone on a journey,
A long way away.
Tell her my heart was too full of farewells –
It is better this way.
Promise me, M'sieur, Cosette will never know . . .

MARIUS I give my word.

VALJEAN . . . what I have spoken, why I must go.

MARIUS For the sake of Cosette, it must be so.

## 7. The Wedding

(MARIUS *and* COSETTE *lead a wedding procession.*)

FIRST CHORUS
Ring out the bells
Upon this day of days

May all the angels
Of the Lord above

In jubilation
Sing their songs of praise

And crown this
Blessed time with
Peace and love.

SECOND CHORUS

Ring out the bells
Upon this day of days

May all the angels
Of the Lord above

In jubilation
Sing their songs of praise

And crown this
Blessed time with
Peace and love.

(*The procession becomes a dancing celebration. A waltz is
  played*)

MAJOR DOMO The Baron and Baroness de Thénard
  wish to pay their respects to the groom!

THENARDIER I forget where we met
Was it not at the Chateau Lafarge,

Where the Duke did that puke
Down the Duchess's de-coll-etage?

MARIUS No, 'Baron de Thénard'
The circles I move in are humbler by far.
Go away, Thénardier!
Do you think I don't know who you are?

MADAME THENARDIER He's not fooled.
Told you so.
Show M'sieur what you've come here to show.
Tell the boy what you know!

MARIUS When I look at you I remember Eponine.
She was more than you deserved, who gave her birth
But now she is with God and happier, I hope,
Than here on earth!

THENARDIER So it goes!
Heaven knows
Life has dealt me some terrible blows!

MADAME THENARDIER You've got cash
And a heart
You could give us a bit of a start!
We can prove, plain as ink,
Your bride's father is not what you think.

THENARDIER There's a tale I could tell . . .

MADAME THENARDIER Information we're willing to
sell . . .

THENARDIER There's a man that he slew!
I saw the corpse clear as I'm seeing you!
What I tell you is true!

MADAME THENARDIER Pity to disturb you at a feast
like this,
But 500 francs surely wouldn't come amiss.

MARIUS In God's name say what you have to say.

THENARDIER But first you pay.

What I saw, clear as light,
Jean Valjean in the sewers that night.
Had this corpse on his back,
Hanging there like a bloody great sack.
I was there, never fear.
Even found me this fine souvenir!

MARIUS I know this! This was mine!
This is surely some heavenly sign!

THENARDIER One thing more. Mark this well.
It was the night that the barricades fell!

MARIUS Then it's true. Then I'm right.
Jean Valjean was my saviour that night!

As for you, take this too!
God forgive us the things that we do!

Come, my love, come, Cossette,
This day's blessings are not over yet!

THENARDIER Ain't it a laugh?
Ain't it a treat?
Hob-nobbin' here
Among the elite?
Here comes a prince,
There goes a Jew,
This one's a queer,
But what can you do?
Paris at my feet,

Paris in the dust,
And here I'm breaking bread
With the upper crust . . .
Beggar at the feast!
Master of the dance!
Life is easy pickings
If you grab your chance.
Everywhere you go
Law-abiding folk
Doing what is decent
But they're mostly broke!
Singing to the Lord on Sundays,
Praying for the gifts he'll send.

M. & MME THENARDIER But we're the ones who
take it.
We're the ones who make it in the end!
Watch the buggers dance,
Watch 'em till they drop,
Keep your wits about you
And you stand on top!
Masters of the land,
Always get your share,
Clear away the barricades
And we're still there!
We know where the wind is blowing,
Money is the stuff we smell.
And when we're rich as Croesus
Jesus! Won't we see you all in Hell!

## 8. Valjean's Room

(VALJEAN *is sitting alone.*)

VALJEAN Alone I wait in the shadows.
I count the hours till I can sleep.
I dreamed a dream Cosette stood by,
It made her weep
To know I die.

Alone, at the end of the day,
Upon this wedding night I pray
Take these children, my Lord, to thy embrace
And show them grace.

God on high,
Hear my prayer.
Take me now
To thy care,
Where you are.
Let me be,
Take me now,
Take me there,
Bring me home,
Bring me home.

| FANTINE | VALJEAN |
|---|---|
| M'sieur, I bless your name. | |
| M'sieur, lay down your burden. | I am ready, Fantine. |
| | At the end of my days. |
| You raised my child in love | |
| And you will be with God. | She's the best of my life. |

(MARIUS *and* COSETTE *burst into the room*)

COSETTE Papa, Papa, I do not understand!
Are you alright? They said you'd gone away.

VALJEAN Cosette, my child, am I forgiven now?
Thank God, thank God, I've lived to see this day.

MARIUS It's you who must forgive a thoughtless fool.
It's you who must forgive a thankless man.
It's thanks to you that I am living
And again I lay down my life at your feet.

Cosette, your father is a saint.
When they wounded me
He took me from the barricade
Carried like a babe,
And brought me home to you!

VALJEAN Now you are here
Again beside me.
Now I can die in peace
For now my life is blessed . . .

COSETTE You will live, Papa, you're going to live.
It's too soon, too soon to say goodbye!

VALJEAN Yes, Cosette, forbid me now to die.
I'll obey,
I will try.
On this page
I write my last confession.
Read it well
When I, at last, am sleeping.
It's a story
Of those who always loved you.
Your mother gave her life for you
Then gave you to my keeping.

FANTINE Come with me
Where chains will never bind you.
All your grief
At last, at last, behind you.
Lord in Heaven
Look down on him in mercy.

VALJEAN Forgive me all my trespasses
And take me to your glory.

VALJEAN, FANTINE, EPONINE Take my hand
And lead me to salvation.

Take my love
For love is everlasting.
And remember
The truth that once was spoken,
To love another person
Is to see the face of God.

ALL Do you hear the people sing
Lost in the valley of the night?
It is the music of a people
Who are climbing to the light.
For the wretched of the earth
There is a flame that never dies.
Even the darkest night will end
And the sun will rise.

They will live again in freedom
In the garden of the Lord.
They will walk behind the plough-share,
They will put away the sword.
The chain will be broken
And all men will have their reward.

Will you join in our crusade?
Who will be strong and stand with me?
Somewhere beyond the barricade
Is there a world you long to see?
Do you hear the people sing?
Say, do you hear the distant drums?
It is the future that they bring
When tomorrow comes!

Will you join in our crusade?
Who will be strong and stand with me?
Somewhere beyond the barricade
Is there a world you long to see?
Do you hear the people sing?
Say, do you hear the distant drums?
It is the future that they bring
When tomorrow comes . . .
Tomorrow comes!

# Picture Credits

---

The photographs between pages 108 and 139 were taken by **Michael Le Poer Trench** at various productions of *Les Misérables* around the world:

'One Day More', original London cast; beginning of Act Two, Vienna; 'On My Own', Los Angeles; the barricade, Toronto; 'Shoot me now or shoot me later', Third National Company, USA; 'Little people know', Australia; 'Give me the spy, Javert', London; 'A Little Fall of Rain', original London cast; 'Bring Him Home', original London cast; Enjolras, Broadway; Enjolras after the death of Gavroche, Vienna; 'So you'd better run for cover', Broadway; death on the barricade, Broadway; death of Enjolras, First National Company, USA; the Paris sewers, Toronto; 'Dog Eat Dog', Norway; Javert and Valjean – the final confrontation, Los Angeles; 'There is no way to go on . . .', London; 'Ring out the bells', Vienna; the wedding ball, Boston; 'My last confession', Australia; 'M'sieur, lay down your burden', Vienna; 'To love another person is to see the face of God', London, 1985; grand finale, Japan.

The author and publishers are grateful to the following for permission to reproduce additional material: Canyon Records, p. 155 top; David Crosswaite, p. 140; Festival Records Pty, p. 157; Hulton-Deutsch, pp. 15, 19, 21 top & bottom, 22, 23, 24, 25, 27, 30 top & bottom, 32, 36, 39, 146; Polydor/Deutschesgrammaphon, p. 154 bottom; Toho Co. Ltd, Japan, pp. 138–9, 144, 145; © Collection Vidlet, p. 42; *Washington Post*, p. 158.

# About the Author

---

Edward Behr is a writer, documentary filmmaker, and contributing editor of *Newsweek*. His books include *The Algerian Problem; Anybody Here Been Raped and Speaks English;* a novel, *Getting Even;* the international best-seller *The Last Emperor,* based on the Bertolucci film; *The Story of Miss Saigon,* cowritten with Mark Steyn; and *Hirohito: Behind the Myth.* His most recent book is *Kiss the Hand You Cannot Bite–The Rise and Fall of the Ceausescus.* Edward Behr lives in France.